A Spiritual Evolution

Nikki Pattillo

OZARK
MOUNTAIN
PUBLISHING

PO Box 754, Huntsville, AR 72740
800-935-0045 or 479-738-2348; fax 479-738-2448
www.ozarkmt.com

Library of Congress Cataloging-in-Publication Data
Pattillo, Nikki 1966-
"A Spiritual Evolution" by Nikki Pattillo
Evolving and ascending into higher dimensions of consciousness through spiritual evolution.
1. Angels 2. Metaphysics 3. New Vibrational Frequencies 4. Spiritual Growth
I. Pattillo, Nikki 1966 - II. Title

Library of Congress Catalog Number: 2011936505
ISBN: 978-1-886940-22-2

Cover Art and Layout by www.noir33.com
Book Design: Julia Degan
Book Set in: Times New Roman
Published by

OZARK
MOUNTAIN
PUBLISHING

PO Box 754
Huntsville, AR 72740

www.ozarkmt.com
Printed in the United States of America

Table of Contents

Acknowledgements

I could not have written this book without specific people being in my life. Thank you to my husband, Charlie, for his unwavering support. You believed in me, my talent, and my psychic abilities and gifts when others did not believe.

To my beautiful daughter Maddy: You are my strength, my courage, my inspiration, and the light at the end of my tunnel.

To my best friend Diane Russo-Cranshaw: Words cannot describe how grateful I was the day that you appeared in my life. Thank you for your unwavering love, support, and giving me some of the happiest moments in my life through your love and laughter.

Lastly, I could not have written this book without my angels and guides who come to me, giving me messages of hope and inspiration to share with all that will walk a spiritual path. I am so grateful to all of them for being with me in this life, protecting me, healing me, loving me, and letting me know I am never alone.

Forward

When I first sat down and started an outline for this book, I knew that my life's purpose included writing and healing. *How could I possibly heal anyone?* I asked the angels over and over. I told my angels that they must be nuts. I couldn't heal myself much less anybody else, and my angels wanted me to write and talk about my journey?

I wasn't sure that I was on the right path when I started this second book. Slowly but surely, ideas started forming about what I should write. I finally realized that information was flowing through me, and I needed to allow it to happen. This was quite an epiphany and made me reflect quite a bit on the world at hand while I wrote.

I realized that we have been going through a spiritual evolution while we are here on Earth. We are not humans on a spiritual journey but, in fact, spiritual beings on a human journey. Throughout time, auras and vibrational frequencies have changed for the better. As time goes on, we are progressing more quickly in this spiritual evolution of our souls while here on Earth.

This book is part of what I have learned from my angels. Not everyone in life can feel happiness, but everyone has and will feel pain. It's what connects us to each other and helps us on our spiritual evolutionary path, so it can't be viewed as a bad thing. What is bad is how we react to the pain in life and whether or not we learn and grow from these spiritual lessons.

Through my own spiritual journey, I have learned my life's purpose and the contribution I am to make to humanity. I have found love and compassion for all people in all walks of life, no matter who they are. Most importantly, I have found an inner peace, serenity, and love in my heart. We can all walk around as angels on Earth feeling the most amazing peace.

Evolving and ascending into higher dimensions of consciousness through our spiritual evolution will always be our goal.

In Love and Light,
Nikki Pattillo

Chapter 1

Ascension

Muddy water, let stand, becomes clear.

~Lau Tzu

We are all ascending to higher dimensions of consciousness and higher vibrational frequencies. If we can say that ascending is evolving, then we can certainly say that ascension is part of our spiritual evolution that has been unfolding throughout history as our energy levels rise on this planet. We are elevating the vibratory rate of our physical and other energetic bodies to the Christ level, whether we realize it or not.

Ascension is also about realizing our God and Goddess selves and creating heaven on Earth. It is about embracing who we really are and dispelling the thought that we are separate from our Creator or the Divine. Ascension is also about bringing the higher and lower aspects of our being into complete harmony and alignment with our higher self or higher purpose. In general, everything in our life that isn't in alignment with our higher purpose tends to fall away with the process of ascension. There can be a difficult period of adjustment during this process, and some of the adjustments we have to make can be hard to view as positive circumstances. This may mean we need to end relationships, move, change jobs, and/or experience further changes that may seem unsettling to us. However, it is necessary for us to release these old patterns to make room for the new higher energy into which we are evolving with each life that we live. The ultimate goal in spiritual ascension is for us to align with a higher source and keep our vibrational frequencies at a higher level to help us live our life's purpose and find the special gifts and talents that we have to offer.

During the process of ascension, we may feel physically exhausted. We might even feel the need to sleep very long hours. Our physical bodies are aligning with the higher vibratory rate of our spiritual bodies to help us facilitate a shift into multi-dimensional awareness, energy, and consciousness.

We may also feel the emotional and mental effects of ascension. They may not be long-lasting, but they do cause a change in our mental state. We might experience sadness and depression, which are feelings that can be part of the alignment process. As we become more centered within ourselves, the world around us may appear more frantic and chaotic for a time.

During ascension, we may experience feelings of emptiness and loneliness, which are part of our complete surrender to our higher self. We will have released the hold of the lower-ego-self and will, therefore, have surrendered to the guidance of our higher-ego-self. These are two levels of the spirit where the lower-ego-self contains the potentials of ego, and the higher-ego-self contains the potentials of the soul.

Once the alignment is complete, we will experience deep feelings of peace. When we have completed our alignments, we will shine like bright stars, and people around us will be able to feel and sense the light that radiates from within us. All of us will be a part of the changes that are occurring here on Earth, and this will help transform the planet and create heaven on Earth.

In order for us to ascend to a place of higher dimensional consciousness, we must become fully conscious. This means stopping old patterns and habits that prevent us from living in heightened awareness. This knowledge or awareness will bring us into the light of higher consciousness. There are many means for bringing various aspects of self into the light of higher awareness, and angels are tirelessly working on this to help us. Prayer, meditation, reading, and practicing good karma are all ways to help us ascend to a higher vibrational frequency.

Living our life's purpose is another way to ascend. Many of us often ask, "What is my life's purpose?" Our life's purpose can be learned by communicating with our angels and guides or by simply allowing our life to be divinely guided so it can unfold into what we are meant to do and who we are meant to be. By raising our vibrational frequencies to higher levels, we can communicate more easily with our higher selves, our guides, and our angels who are here loving us and helping us to discover or remember our life's purpose.

For most of us here on Earth, it can take up to half our lifetime to *wake up* to the fact that we have a mission to help this Earth. The feeling of *something is coming* or an idea of a *big mission* is quite common among people at this time. We often feel we are supposed to be doing more than we are currently doing; we just don't know what that big mission is.

What is a big mission? A big mission is some significant event that all of us have for our life—something that has a major impact on humanity or Earth, either negative or positive, depending on our spiritual advancement, position, and influence in life. The big mission can be any one of an infinite number of things, but it is different for every one of us, and in some way it makes a huge and lasting impact in the world that we do not always realize at the moment it happens.

For example, for some of us the *big mission* might be missionary work for a period of time or healing work, or it might be talking a teenager out of committing suicide, perhaps without even knowing it. Those of us who are aware and conscious of our spiritual power and light are sensing the emerging quickening of time and energy in this three-dimensional world. Our feelings of wanting or needing to begin our mission or purpose here on Earth are becoming stronger with our ascension.

Ascension also brings about the expansion of our auric field and our chakras. This can be very tiring for us. It is common for those of us that are ascending to need as much as nine to twelve hours of sleep or downtime per night. Ascension can be very demanding on our energy when we are trying to elevate our energy and dimensional consciousness.

The process of ascension will allow us to be treated as the unique souls that we are. This is because newer and higher vibrational frequencies allow us to see that we are all one, and we are all rowing the same boat, so to speak. This new energy transition is also being born through our children as souls who have been coming to Earth on a group mission to help us in our ascension. Each year, more and more of these enlightened souls are affecting the ascension process of whole communities by their energies and their auric fields, whether they realize it or not.

Parents of today are setting the foundation for rearing spiritually aware children. They're doing this by clearing their own negative energies and old emotions to help their children with their ascension. The old ways, or the teaching and parenting skills that are on the old energy grid, will slowly begin to change in the years and decades to come. Those who do not raise their vibrational frequencies to align with the ascending planet, people, and lightworkers will not be able to handle the new higher frequencies here on Earth and will become ill.

Ascension will make it possible for all life to blossom and for all of us to manifest our dreams, live our life's purpose, and experience the life intended for each and every one of us. In time, we will live our lives with compassion, love, respect, and a value of wholeness and oneness. Living and recognizing the Law of One—that we are all connected to each other—is a common theme with people today. This is because conscious awareness is an important part of ascension.

Currently, many lightworkers on this planet are working to help us transition to a higher vibrational frequency and a new Earth by raising awareness and consciousness. Through their very presence, they are forcing us to wake up to who we are and what we are doing to ourselves and to our planet. They do this as spiritual warriors who live their truth and make us aware of ours.

For these beings of higher consciousness, incarnating on planet Earth at this time is an adventure. It is a group project in which millions of lightworkers are arriving as teachers and healers for humanity. They are here to awaken us and do whatever they need to do to shock us into the reality that if we don't change our ways, we are going to "hell in a hand basket." We are digging a hole so deep that we may soon never find our way out.

Lightworkers that are here helping us don't see their mission in a heavy and responsible way. For this reason, some are quite often under-prepared and run into trouble with our outdated systems and beliefs. We need to recognize and understand why they are here helping us and let them know that we are hearing them and are willing to help with their mission of conscious evolution through our thoughts, words, and actions.

The purpose of conscious evolution for us and our Earth as a whole is to create awareness. With the assistance of lightworkers we, as a civilization, will rediscover our oneness, our common humanity.

The knowledge we are gaining through ascension and our spiritual evolution can be used to raise our consciousness and create a new Earth. This will be a place where all of us can thrive and be respected for who we are and where we will learn to respect everyone's similarities and differences as we live among one another with loving tolerance. In fact, we can celebrate the incredible diversity that characterizes our *oneness* as that which makes life an adventure in consciousness. From this celebration, we can develop loving tolerance for the diversity in our world. Without this loving tolerance of diversity, we will have no peace.

Lightworkers and teachers of conscious awareness that have been arriving on Earth over the last decade are spiritual warriors who are assisting us by clearing old systems and outdated beliefs so that new systems and beliefs can be created. They are the *systems-busters* who will liberate us from our old ways of thinking.

Lightworkers do this by incarnating into our families and communities. They bring with them their gifts of advanced spiritual development, higher levels of consciousness, and wisdom. They are spiritually aware and awake and refuse to allow themselves to be constrained or enslaved by impersonal systems. They show us that gentle, wise, and high-level beings cannot flourish and thrive in the systems we have created. They have come to teach us about tolerance for all living and non-living things, respect for others, and how to care for our home—this planet.

Lightworkers function at an extremely high level of consciousness, and they are overly sensitive both to their environments and to the feelings and emotions of others. Every thought that we have, every word that we speak, whether it is silently to ourselves or aloud to others, either adds to or takes away from the light of humanity. There are no insignificant thoughts or words—each one has energy and an effect. When our thoughts and words come from a place of unconditional love, which means that they are without judgment, they spread light and increase the light and vibrational frequency on the planet. But when they come from fear or anger, they take away from the light. Yes, our thoughts and words do make a difference, and each one is important. Each person is as important as another in spreading the light to others. Even our smallest judgmental thought has an effect on our world and all living things on it. These feelings block our energy and keep us at a lower vibrational frequency on the old energy grid that keeps us from ascending.

Learning to let go of old, ineffective and disharmonious energy patterns and adapting to change is also important for ascension. Reaction to change is often tinged with suspicion, caution, or resistance, and adapting to change almost always involves give and take. We have to let go of something to gain something. Holding onto old emotions or old energy can block our energy and slow us down.

On a spiritual level, bad emotions and issues can also block energy. Often we have old issues tying up emotional fields and energy, and our minds, bodies, and spirits don't want to take on more issues. We are overloaded with stuff, so to speak. As a result, the subconscious finds every excuse as to why we should not deal with emotional issues and fears surrounding old negative energy patterns. Realizing core issues and releasing old and outdated emotional issues will help us improve our energy patterns.

When understanding ascension, it is important that we also understand the process of forgiveness. Forgiveness allows us to release old pain that will allow current issues in our lives to suddenly seem not seem so overwhelming. We allow old emotions to be released when we release our expectations both towards ourselves and the world around us, which makes room for new and balanced energy.

If we think of the emotional body or auric field like a hard drive, there is only so much memory it can hold before it starts to freeze up. Releasing these old programs and pains from the past makes room for better, newer programs to be installed.

Forgiveness is the foundation of all spiritual work and growth. If we are able to allow forgiveness to sit within our hearts, then great beauty and opportunity are within everyone with ascension, even those with old scars and betrayals buried deep within them. Forgiveness is not a process of giving something to another person who may not deserve it but is, instead, a process of turning our energy inward and using the power of love to examine our relationships within ourselves and others. When we are anchored in forgiveness, we are all within the spiritual realm of conscious awareness rather than in the realm of emotions or the mind.

It is natural to release old energy because holding onto it hinders the flow of love into our own lives and blocks our own spiritual balance and peace. Love is the energy that gives and maintains life. Forgiving others, even those who don't seem to deserve it, can bring life-giving energy into our body. Love is the emotion that binds us to each other.

The issues that seem to defy forgiveness are always about love—love that we never received, love offered but rejected or betrayed, or love used as manipulation or control. By tying up our spiritual energy reserves into old hurts, we are limiting the vibrational energy of love available in the present moment. Each morning or evening can be spent reviewing emotions or hurts from the day that we are carrying around, working through them, and letting them go from our spiritual light.

We all have old energy in our auras and in our heart chakras that create challenges and blockages in our lives that can hold us back from the process of ascension. We are all in the process of learning how to clear these issues, entities, thought forms, fears, and old wounds from our bodies so that we can all ascend and become the enlightened beings that we are meant to be.

Lightworkers are teaching us that ascension can also come through faith. Great teachers of the world, such as Buddha, derived strength and inspiration not from muscle or intellect but from faith. Buddha spoke a great language that went straight to people's hearts. We, as a civilization or humanity, are no different. These teachings connect us through our heart chakras and ask us to have faith.

Hollywood child star, Shirley Temple Black, once narrated an incident in her biography about her husband, Charles, and his mother. When Charles was a boy, he asked his mom what was the happiest moment in her life.

His mother replied, "This moment, right now."

The boy further asked, "But what about all the other happy moments in your life, say, when you were married?"

His mother replied, "My happiest moment then was then. My happiest moment now is now. You can live your life only in the moment you are in, and this requires unflinching faith."

Through faith, we can see that the mission of lightworkers is to teach us to be a light not only to ourselves but also to others who can't, won't, or don't know how to hold the light for themselves. They are here at this critical time in humanity's spiritual evolution to build and spread the light for all of humanity.

We can be a light and spread our light by focusing our intention on what we want in life. When we focus on what others have, we are seeing our lives from a point of lack. By focusing our energies on what we have, we bring the light into our life and, in return, can spread this light to others. Each of us is important and our energy is continuously manifested all around us. We can take this power and use it wisely, for each of us has come to spread the light to the world. If we use it well, we can create heaven on Earth through ascension for ourselves and for all of humanity.

Chapter 2
Reincarnation

Who says the eternal being does not exist? Who says the sun has gone out? Someone who climbs up on the roof and closes his eyes tight and says, 'I don't see anything.'

~ Jalalu'l-din Rumi

Reincarnation is an anglicized word of the Latin derivation meaning *reinfleshment,* the coming again of a soul into a human body. Reincarnation also comes from the Hindu-Buddhist philosophy of soul transmigration. This is the belief of the birth-death-birth cycle where a soul moves from one body to another for many lifetimes. Each new body or life is the direct result of the quality of life the soul led in a previous life. Thus, a good life results in rebirth to a higher quality of life, and a bad life results in rebirth to a lower quality of life. Reincarnation is almost exclusively about previous existences and a soul's spiritual growth.

The quality of lives led through reincarnation is based on the Law of Karma, a central foundation of Hinduism and other Eastern-based philosophies. Karma teaches that good thoughts, actions, and deeds are rewarded and bad thoughts, actions, and deeds are punished. The ultimate goal in the karmic cycle is for a soul to progress to the highest level of existence and become one with the Divine.

To accomplish this spiritual progression, each person lives a series of lives in different physical bodies, coming back over and over again in order to progress through his/her spiritual lessons. This is reincarnation, part of the process on the path to enlightenment.

All souls can be considered eternal when evaluating past, present, and future lives because the soul itself is eternal. To advance in spiritual lessons and awareness, we reincarnate into a series of physical bodies to experience different existences. Throughout our many lifetimes, we can reincarnate as both sexes and all races, have various socio-economic backgrounds, and practice many religions. This continued cycle from one life to another ends when our soul's education and lessons are complete. If we haven't achieved that, we will return to Earth to reap the results of all our thoughts, actions, and deeds and to gain further knowledge and wisdom as we journey toward spiritual mastery.

Thus we are born to achieve this state of complete balance in our mental, physical, and spiritual bodies. When all of our lessons are completed, there will no longer be the need for us to reincarnate in physical form since we will have progressed enough to move to other forms and lessons.

As souls, we move *forward* because spiritual progression isn't a hierarchy but more like a train where our souls are located in various places on this train. The ultimate goal is for us to advance to the front of the train where we can join or be one with the Divine.

During the pre-planning stages of our reincarnation, there is a place in the spiritual plane where our soul goes to meet with our angels, guides, and a planning committee to choose our bodies and lives for our next reincarnation. This place looks like a spherical dome with what appears to be TV-like screens from floor to ceiling. On these screens are pictures of future persons in various stages of their lives. We select from the bodies and lives available during this life selection process.

We are able to enter into a body in any of the screens shown to us and experience what is taking place in that life for a few moments. We are able to see, hear, and feel that life, which will help us determine which scenarios will be best for our spiritual growth. Sometimes we will choose a life that will help another soul with his/her karmic debt. For example, we may choose to marry someone and die within a few years of that marriage, so our spouse or partner would feel the loss of someone that he/she loved deeply in order to pay a karmic debt from a previous life. We also have several choices in the manner in which we could die. It may be from a disease, drowning, or a car crash. Our choice will be made wisely for the spiritual growth of all involved.

Our passing is not necessarily set in stone. If we chose to die in a car crash, there might be a chance that we wouldn't plan to be in a car in a certain place at a certain time for the crash to occur but would feel the impulse to do so because we picked this exit. Our higher self, angels, and guides are always working behind the scenes because specific life's objectives may change during the course of our life. Then our life could be altered to fit the new goals and objectives if circumstances changed due to free-will actions during that life.

Souls are able to visit the Akashic records while on the spiritual plane and since we live in cycles of reincarnation, we are able to study the past before returning to physical form. The Akashic records are libraries containing the records of every soul from birth to death in every lifetime. They are the spiritual learning centers where souls can view the "what ifs" and "should haves" of past lives. Spiritual advancement can still be made after a soul crosses over, just not as quickly as living a life here on Earth or in some other universe. Though we can learn things by reading books, we can learn much more if we are actually the characters in the book, not the bystanders. For example, an individual could read a book about bravery but unless that individual jumped in front of an oncoming car to save a child, he/she would never know the true meaning or feeling of this emotion.

It is because of this type of learning process used for our spiritual development that we live one truth. The truth is that our soul comes back over and over to pay karmic debts, learn spiritual lessons, and to reach a point of advancement where we become one with the Divine. We will keep reincarnating as long as we need until we reach all our spiritual goals. This is the one truth regardless of whatever we feel we have done right or wrong in our lives, whatever we believe to be true or not in our lives, or whatever wrongs we feel have undeservingly come to us.

It is the trials and tribulations we experience in our lives that make us grow spiritually and advance toward becoming more loving beings. It isn't our actual belief in reincarnation that is the proof that it really exists, but the ability we have to remember past life experiences and bring past life knowledge, wisdom, and skills into our current life that is the actual proof.

The challenges that we choose in each life also come to us through our DNA. It is a kind of hereditary boomerang of energy that comes from our parents that give us our lessons we need to work on in a particular life although challenges can come from all directions if we are not learning our lessons. When called on, our angels and guides will always help us to achieve our spiritual lesson checklist, so to speak, and will never give up on us.

An example of this inherited energy might include a case of an abusive parental relationship. We may come into the world being physically and verbally abused by a parent and, in turn, may or may not become a physically and emotionally abusive parent. This abuse may be part of our karma coming from a previous life or just part of a spiritual lesson for us or another member of our soul group. Whatever the case may be, some of our spiritual lessons can be very difficult.

We have the innate ability to change our vibrational frequency to make sure we reincarnate into a much better life next time we are here. This can be done by stopping our cycles or breaking our habits. Learning, growing, becoming aware and, most importantly, being grateful for our lessons are the most crucial tasks in each life that we live.

Due to the difficulty of our lessons, it could take many lifetimes for us to learn just a lesson or two. Just as we aren't able to earn a college degree in one month, it may take many lifetimes to achieve all of our spiritual goals. A lesson may be much more difficult for one soul than another. For example, it may take one soul thirty lifetimes to conquer the emotion of envy and another soul just one. It isn't a race, but if we become more aware, we can progress more quickly.

Often members of our soul group will agree to come with us into a life to help us learn our lesson or lessons. For example, many members of one soul group could be concerned with communication and teaching, another with healing, another with courage, and another with self-acceptance. They could incarnate together as a family, friends, or business associates to work on one or all of these issues. There can be similar ideals, aspirations, likes and dislikes, so there can be common ground to connect us all while on Earth.

A soul group can work together for more than one lifetime. It is also possible for them to be involved in the decision-making processes regarding future lifetimes. They can also assist us in reviewing our achievements in a lifetime that has just passed. Our soul group is always there for us even though not all the members of the group will reincarnate at the same time. Those members who are not reincarnated may act as spiritual guides during the physical life of the soul or souls who are living on Earth at any particular time.

They can visit us in dreams, inspire us with thoughts, or, in some cases, speak to us directly during meditation. Whether it is our soul group, angels, or guides, our *team* will help guide us through this difficult three-dimensional world and help us to stay on track with our lessons. This Earth is an incredibly tough playground but develops souls in a way that cannot be found in other universes. Souls that chose to reincarnate on Earth become some of the most advanced souls around.

In the end, we come here over and over to learn our lessons and to act as spiritual growth-seeking souls. Before entering each lifetime, we make agreements with as few as one soul or perhaps as many as twenty souls. We agree on what we will offer one another and how we will help each other with our lessons. These souls can be our children, our best friend, husband, wife, worst enemy, boss, business partner, or even the schoolteacher that encouraged us with patience and kindness. Since we have free will, we may create a path that takes us in many different directions, and this is why we have to make various agreements with so many others.

The universe works on the principle of energy. Our family and friends, who may be in the same soul group, may have similar vibrational frequencies as we do. Looking at lessons being learned by family and friends may help us reach within and look at our own life's lessons.

For example, in quite a few lifetimes, Gayle has struggled with powerlessness in the physical realm. Her struggle led her into abusive relationships where her low self-esteem was reinforced. On the other hand in several lifetimes, Mary had difficulties in valuing herself, and so she controlled people through anger and abuse to feel in control of childhood issues that left her scarred.

When Gayle and Mary coordinated their lives, they set up a strong probability to meet. Their intention was that Gayle and Mary would become best friends and work together on resolving their respective issues. In her relationship with an abuser, Gayle would learn that she must begin to make choices that would reflect her self-worth. Mary, on the other hand, needed to learn that she could not possess or control anyone, especially through anger, for power must be felt and come from within the spirit and be used for good.

Mary would be an abuser like Gayle's husband so she could see how his actions, similar to hers, affect people. Gayle could gain inner strength from Mary, learn to stand up for herself, and thus gain self-worth and self-love through Mary's example of strength, albeit misdirected in an abusive manner. Due to free will, Gayle may find herself challenged during the course of her life where she can choose to value herself. If Gayle's vibrational frequency would change, it could help Mary change her vibrational frequency as well. Mary could learn from Gayle what emotional abuse does to a person and stop her abusive cycle.

Due to free-will choices that are not made with awareness and consciousness, it may be that neither Gayle nor Mary would be able to achieve all or any of their spiritual lessons. If that is so, then a different combination may be played out in another life. Or, specific situations may be re-arranged during their current life to help them along. It is important to note here that the harshness of our lessons may be influenced by our primary guides. A particular guide may help a soul achieve his/her lessons softly and easily, which may extend the number of lifetimes it takes to learn these lessons. On the other hand, another guide may set up harsher situations to make sure a particular soul learns his/her lessons more quickly in fewer lives. In both of these scenarios, the soul would agree to the ease or harshness of these lessons before coming to Earth. We know what we are getting into before we come as it has all been carefully planned and arranged.

In the end, we will have to view and review all aspects of our last life with our guides and soul groups. We review every decision, action, thought, and word, both good and bad. There will be karmic debts to pay if we did not live a life with kindness, tolerance, and, most importantly, consciousness and awareness.

When reviewing each life, we will see there are many people who have had an impact on it. All of these people are our soul mates. They love us dearly and are all working together toward one goal—to help us learn our spiritual lessons with love and compassion in our hearts.

Ultimately, we are all connected to our soul group and to each other. Through this connection, our goals, purposes, experiences, and vibrational frequencies are all shared. These connections on Earth do not automatically indicate that we have met before on the physical plane. We may never have met on the physical plane, but we may know each other from the spiritual plane.

It is thought that more time is spent on the spiritual plane than in physical form. A soul can spend up to hundreds of Earth years on the spiritual plane before reincarnating again, although it is not likely. In the spiritual world, we have friends in very much the same way that we have friends on Earth. Some friends are close to us, others are intimately known to us, and still others are just acquaintances. Friendships in the spiritual world have nothing to do with liking or not liking one another—it has to do with the level of spiritual advancement we have achieved, and these are the soul groups with whom we are associated.

It is important to note here that it is not uncommon for a soul to come from a completely different soul group in order to help another group that may not be advancing as they should. They may reincarnate with another soul group in order to act as their guides here on Earth and help them along.

It is also possible for a soul to move to another more advanced group more quickly than other souls in the group. Some may advance together while in others, one or two may move on more quickly. It is all about the spiritual advancement we make with each life that we live.

For example, we may be connected to a group of souls who are working on karma. For these lessons, we may choose to return later than the rest of our group, so we probably wouldn't complete all our lessons in one lifetime. Or, we may move on at a faster pace than our group and decide to progress by choosing harsher lives where we learn our lessons more quickly but only if we live that life consciously and in awareness. Another choice could be to remain with the group and become a leader or teacher, assisting them in their progression. This, in turn, helps us to progress even further because there is much to be learned while teaching.

The possibilities are endless, and the choice is always ours to make with the assistance and guidance from our angels and guides. If we decide to move on, we will join another group or perhaps work with one or two other souls. Our work with other souls may last one Earth day, an entire lifetime, or several hundred lifetimes. We choose all of these relationships, and each relationship is based on the cooperation and desire to spiritually progress or assist others in their lessons.

For the creation of a physical family, the younger less-experienced souls will tend to team up with souls that are very closely related to them. These souls will often swap roles with one another from lifetime to lifetime, sometimes being the child, at other times the parent, at one time the female, or at another time the male. The familiarity of the souls helps each individual progress more quickly. It is to be noted that we do tend to come back as a particular sex. For example, a soul may be female in 80% of his/her lives because his/her karmic lessons may be learned more quickly as that particular gender.

When we as souls first enter the physical plane, it may seem to be hostile to us. We can be confused and wary of the physical body and be very susceptible to lower vibrational energies. As a result, our angels will help place us in circumstances where we are guided and supported. The universe is loving and supportive; therefore, it creates feelings of security by surrounding us with people with whom we are very familiar. However, as with everything in the universe, this is only in general. It is not a hard and fast rule that older, more advanced souls might be part of a group of less experienced souls so that they can help the younger souls on their new journeys.

Many older souls may choose to be born into families where perhaps only one member is well-known to them and possibly from their own soul group. This is because older souls are more concerned with introspective spiritual advancement. They may be preparing to teach or to become leaders in one field or another, and the experience of feeling like *the odd one out* will lead them toward self-examination. Instead of getting caught up with the function and duty of a family, these souls will often seem to be the black sheep or viewed as different or eccentric by other members of their family. These circumstances may lead to difficult personal challenges because the lessons are almost always internal rather than external.

It is important to note that not all souls that are here on Earth at this time are living in cycles of reincarnation during Earth's energy shifts. Many souls have agreed to come and help our planet at this time. If you had a neighbor that you knew was going to commit suicide, you would certainly feel a moral obligation to talk to him/her and try to help that person. This is similar to what is happening to lightworkers that are here helping Earth. We are slowly annihilating our Earth and can't seem to stop our old habits, ways of doing things, and outdated beliefs. Lightworkers have come here from all areas of the universe to try and help us and our Earth. Some have not incarnated on this planet but instead have been downloaded with information from the Akashic records of other souls chosen by a council.

If you were to go to Hawaii, you would certainly go to the library, buy a book, or look up information on the web about the land, its people, where to go, etc. It is the same with lightworkers who are here helping us. They have been downloaded with others' information who have been here before. They may even have downloads of many past-life experiences that are not their own. This information is used to help these lightworkers who have never incarnated on this particular planet. They are downloaded with this information so the knowledge and gifts they are bringing can be used more effectively and efficiently.

For the rest of us, knowing and understanding our past lives is helpful in understanding our spiritual lessons, and it is imperative that we concentrate on our current life. While past-life experiences can help us understand why we are here, it is in our current life where our spiritual progression or spiritual evolution is currently taking place and needs our attention. While we can bring abilities in from previous incarnations and we can learn from past mistakes, the current life is where our immediate lessons and karma are being played out.

Although reincarnation is about spiritual advancement, it is important to note that the spiritual realm is not a hierarchy. We may have heard about reincarnation being compared to a tapestry where all of our lives are like interwoven threads in continuous lines with others' lives. One thread always affects another to form an intricate picture or lesson. Together this tapestry creates a picture of how connected we all are to one another.

The spiritual realm isn't like a hierarchy but like a train where the Divine or Great One is the conductor at the front of the train. The great ones, angels, and guides are all in cars further back on the train. As progressing souls of light, we are all located somewhere along this train. The sooner we can learn to connect to our spirits and live our lives like angels walking on Earth, the sooner we can move *forward* on this beautiful train of light. By living our lives consciously and in gratitude for every living and non-living thing in this world, we will all be able to move more quickly to the front of the train to be one with the Divine. We do this by mastering our lessons with each reincarnation cycle that we live.

Chapter 3
Karma

One of the most difficult things is not to change society—but to change yourself.

~Nelson Mandela

*K*arma is a Sanskrit word from the root "Kri," which means to make or to do. Karma simply means *action*. It operates in the universe as the continuous chain reaction of cause and effect. Karma means that "as you sow, so shall you reap" in this and any other lifetime until we understand the complete consequences of all our actions. Karma is the universal law of cause and effect, action and reaction, total cosmic justice, and personal responsibility. "A good cause, a good effect; a bad cause, a bad effect" is a common saying when referring to karma. Karma works on both action and thought, and this is why it is important for us to train our mind to think positive thoughts no matter what situations we encounter along our life's journeys.

Karma is also the sum of a person's actions in this and previous lives. While on Earth, we as souls live in the worlds of reincarnation and karma. Karma is justice. It does not reward or punish and shows no favoritism. The purpose of karma is to maintain balance in the universe. In order for that balance to be maintained, living beings must learn their spiritual lessons and learn to live consciously and responsibly with an open mind that extends beyond just us. An open mind begins the path to enlightenment, and enlightenment brings greater understanding of all living and non-living things around us.

According to Janarrdhana Guptha in New Age information, there are four different types of karma that a soul works on in life:

1. **Sanchita Karma**: Sanchita karma is the *sum total* or *accumulated actions* karma. It is the accumulated result of all our actions from all our past lifetimes. In every moment of every day, we either are adding to or reducing this type of karma. Sanchita karma is the vast store of karma accumulated in all previous births that has yet to be resolved. This is our total cosmic debt, and it is waiting to be fulfilled in our future births. So unless and until the Sanchita karma of a soul is cleared, it will remain with us in each new physical body in order to exhaust its balance.

2. **Prarabdha Karma**: Prarabdha karma is considered *fructifying karma* or the idea of an "action beginning and being set in motion." This is the portion of our karma that our soul works on in our present life. If we work down our agreed-upon debt in this lifetime, then more past debts surface and can be worked on as well. This is how Prarabdha karma gets dissolved.

3. **Aagami Karma**: Aagami karma is our *future* karma. It is the karmic map that is coming as a result of the merits and demerits of the present thoughts, actions, and words of our current birth. It is the portion of actions in the present life that can add to or subtract from our Sanchita karma or cosmic karma. If we fail to work off our debt, then more debts are added to Aagami karma and are brought forward to work off in future lives.

4. **Kriyamana Karma**: Kriyamana karma is the daily, *instant* karma created in this life that is worked off immediately. These are debts that are created and then dissipated or balanced in a timely manner. For example, if we do something wrong, we get caught and we might spend time in jail. It is karma that is right in front of us to decide or act upon and can contribute and/or influence our immediate future karma in an important way.

As souls, we experience constant cycles of births and deaths into a series of bodies until we have learned all the spiritual lessons that the totality of all our experiences have to teach us. Every day we are working on these experiences via physical and spiritual forces in the universe. Physical, spiritual, and mental thoughts and actions are never lost but are transformed and played out through our soul's karma.

Through our thoughts, actions, and words, we are releasing spiritual energy to the universe and are, in turn, affected by influences or energies coming in to us from all directions. We are our own sender and receiver of our thoughts and actions. As we sow, so shall we reap in this or any other lifetime. Any of our physical actions or thoughts can change our energy. Bad actions and thoughts create bad energy; good actions and thoughts create good energy. The circumstances created by these energy patterns are played out through a karmic balance sheet.

Our character is dependent on good thoughts, actions, and words. When we have thoughts, these have an effect on our circumstances and, therefore, our karma. For example, if we hit someone, we may cause harm, pain, or injury to the person, and the law of karma requires us to experience the same pain. This happens so we learn to behave in a way that causes good experiences to others and especially to ourselves.

In some circumstances, we may also attract people who have the same or similar karma that we have. If we physically fight others, we may attract this type of individual over and over. Until we become aware and conscious of our own behavior and want to change it, we will stay in the same karmic pattern. Until we start to strive for change and a more peaceful environment, we will be stuck in bad karmic cycles, repeating them until our spiritual lessons are learned.

The law of karma affects all that is, including friends, families, cities, and even countries. It also affects all that we do toward anyone or anything—including humans, animals, plants, planets, and beings of any nature. Every action, thought, and emotion is energy, and this radiates into the universe like a radio station. Some people may radiate thoughts and feelings of love that raise their vibrational frequency. Some may cause mental or emotional stress to others that may cause mental or emotional pain, which lowers their vibrational frequency.

All this energy is constantly rippling through the universe. Our thoughts and emotions, no matter how private we may consider them, affect others around us. We are a result of the energy we create from our thoughts and actions, which, again, contributes to our karmic balance sheet. This energy is also part of our aura and affects everything around us, including our family, friends, the world, and even the universe.

Being aware of all our thoughts and emotions, as well as all our words and actions, will help us to create positive energy in our lives. We must be prepared to receive the kind of energy we radiate both physically and in our thoughts and minds. Thoughts of violence or punishment toward others may hurt people just as much as any physical violence and may come back as a karmic boomerang. Thoughts of love and good will towards others will bring us good karma. If we are kind to all, even those who are not kind to us, we will find true happiness and will be able to create good karma, as well as work off any balances we have created in our current lives or brought forth from past lives.

Since thoughts are just as important as actions with regard to karma, these thoughts can be made more effective by meditating. If we throw a stone into a stormy ocean with rough waves, we probably won't be able to see any ripples made by that stone. Think of the stone as a thought and the stormy ocean as our minds filled with clutter. If the stone/thought is tossed into a stormy ocean/cluttered mind, the effects of the stone landing in the rough water could not be seen. However, if we were to calm that stormy ocean or our mind like a peaceful, calm pond, and we threw the stone or thought into it, the ripples would be seen to the very edge of the pond. By calming our minds and thinking peaceful or happy thoughts, the effects or ripples from these tranquil and contented thoughts can be felt by all.

Mary T. Browne states in her book, *The Power of Karma*, that the law of karma cannot be separated from the doctrine of reincarnation. Reincarnation tells us that we live not one life but many. We return to Earth over and over until we have achieved *perfection* through our own labor. Perfection is a state of total selflessness. All desire for physical pleasures is replaced by a complete dedication to serve humanity. We are, in essence, a composite of all our lives but must first learn to focus on how best to live the present one. The law of karma is very simple. It states, "Whatever you do to others will be done to you in this or any future incarnation of your soul."

Karma and reincarnation are completely interwoven. Each one of us is making karma, good or bad, in every thought, action, and word we produce. Reincarnation and our lives in the physical realm of Earth give us the schoolroom to balance our karma and, ultimately, to learn and achieve self-mastery or spiritual perfection. Through a series of lives, we are given the opportunity to shape ourselves into beautiful, peaceful, fulfilled, loving, and selfless individuals. Past experiences not remembered are never really lost. They are part of our minds and exist in feelings, attractions, tastes, dispositions, and knowledge that can be accessed at any time.

As we live in cycles of reincarnation and karma, there is no such thing as death. Life is a continuation, not a termination. We *pass* from the physical world to the spiritual world with all the experiences gained throughout a succession of lives. Although lessons are still being learned in the spiritual realm, our souls rest in this realm until we're ready to return to Earth, gather more knowledge, and learn more lessons. Then we return to a physical body in order to proceed with our education, spiritual evolution, and further balance our personal karma.

Frequently, people know nothing of the purpose and the impending enfoldment of karma. There is good reason for this. Often people operate out of fear. If we consciously knew that an intensely painful karmic debt was about to occur with someone, we would run as fast as possible in the opposite direction, thus avoiding the repayment or the lesson that our soul previously agreed to experience. If the situation was avoided, then the karmic debt would not be paid. This is why we often don't always remember who we are and why we're here. In some circumstances, this knowledge may inhibit our spiritual growth and evolution.

Karma is not fate. Fate is a notion of predestination. Karma is specifically chosen with the purpose of undergoing a learning experience. This means we may find ourselves pulled to people or situations for a reason. Because of free will and various types of karma, our paths can be altered while we are living here on Earth. We will have many chances to learn our spiritual lessons since opportunities are presented to us on a regular basis. With these opportunities come karmic points, both good and bad. The more we are aware, grow, and learn our spiritual lessons, the more our lives can be altered for the better.

As mentioned earlier, the laws of reincarnation and karma affect people, families, cities, and even nations. They can last a few seconds, such as a short intense pain. Other times karma can last a whole lifetime, such as having a kind grandmother who looked after us for many years. In other scenarios, a foe can cause us the loss of our leg early in life, or we can have a handicap that can last for decades. The length of the karmic experience in some circumstances can be in direct proportion to the length of the original karmic incident. If we deprive someone of the use of his/her legs for twenty years, then this can become a twenty-year karmic debt. If we cut short someone's life by one year, then our own life can be cut short by one year in this or a later life. If we raise an orphan with kindness and generosity for twelve years, then we can be repaid with twelve years of kindness because what we give comes back to us. However, due to Kriyamana karma, it is possible to shorten the length of a karmic debt. Through service to humanity and to Earth, bad karmic debts can be paid off more quickly.

It is important to note here that a mental or physical handicap may not necessarily be due to a karmic debt. It may be a great spiritual lesson being learned. Some brave souls agree to assume additional hardships to progress more quickly in a single lifetime. By choosing a life where an individual may be considered *different*, maybe handicapped in some way, a soul can make great spiritual strides and advancement. It is difficult having additional hardships because Earth is such a tough playground. It is important to see people with additional challenges in their lives as the wonderful and brave souls that they are.

Souls may even have chosen to come in groups to teach humanity lessons. This is true of 9/11. Specific souls chose to pass on during this horrific event to help raise our awareness about fear. After 9/11 many people said, "I am *not* afraid of terrorists. I will not let this extreme group scare me." It is important during this time to not hold fear in our hearts. Fear is a highly contagious emotion that does not serve humanity in any form. It is also what isolates our planet and keeps other beings in the universe from interacting with us.

Those who have chosen a specific sexual orientation in our world compose another group of souls who are presently helping humanity at this time. When we see or hear about men marrying men or women marrying women, we are reminded that we should never judge others but be accepting and keep love, tolerance, and respect for all living things on this planet in our hearts. Neither hate nor fear has a place in this world; in addition, these emotions do not serve any positive karmic circumstance in any form. We should all live by the Law of One with loving tolerance for all people in all walks of life on our Earth. These brave souls are here challenging and allowing us to have many opportunities to raise our vibrational frequency and add good karma to our lives.

Karma is all about universal balance. What goes around comes around; we reap what we sow. Each moment of life gives us the opportunity to become more balanced, to create new good karma, and to take another step on the path toward self-mastery. This process moves us from our past lives, through our current lives, and into our future lives. Despite the fact that we cannot change the past, the future is ours to shape. There is comfort in knowing there's always another chance. It's important to be aware of who we are and why we are here because our thoughts, words, and actions put coins into either our *good karma piggy bank* or our *bad karma piggy bank*.

There are twelve rules of karma that help govern life on Earth:

1. **Karma teaches us responsibility.** Karma is determined by unselfish intentions and motivations; it teaches us how to behave more responsibly and how to be co-creators of our own destinies. The goal of karma is to give us all the experiences that we need to evolve into greater levels of love, joy, awareness, and responsibility. Karma teaches us that we are completely responsible for all circumstances of our lives. Karma is like training wheels that keep us on the straight and narrow path until we have mastered our vehicle and can ride freely on our own.

2. **Karma is a non-punishing force.** It is very important for us to understand that karma is not a system of punishment put in place by a higher authority. The common misconception is that the laws of karma operate in such a manner as to punish us for

our so-called wrongdoings. The punishment is always self-inflicted from a karmic point of view. Karma acts on a living entity based on its previous actions. This counteraction allows us to be placed in a situation where we understand why our previous choices and actions were mistakes. We learn best through experience, and this is what karma does—it puts us in places and circumstances where we experience spiritual lessons first hand.

3. **Karma teaches us to learn our lessons.** The main reason for reincarnating is to learn our spiritual lessons and to advance spiritually. Reincarnation and karma are thus interrelated. However, this does not apply to those who choose to reincarnate to teach others and help them to grow spiritually. Before we reincarnate, we choose the circumstances, parents, social conditions, and situations into which we are born in order to give us the ideal conditions for learning the lessons that we have set out to learn in this lifetime. This means that our current family genetics and psychological environments are not mainly responsible for our psychological makeup. They are only the vehicles for the expression of our soul and serve to bring about the interplay of factors required for the natural unfolding of our karmic circumstances.

4. **Karma is neither good nor bad.** Karma operates on universal laws, which create total justice. Karma is very impersonal, and it applies to everyone at all times—without exception. Karma makes us realize that we are all interrelated, irrespective of our nationality, religion, race, creed, sex, etc., and thereby teaches us the Law of One—that we are all connected to each other. Karma also teaches us to take ownership of ourselves as it makes us responsible for our actions in all aspects of our lives. Karma gives us an

understanding of the cause and effect of these actions, whether they are good or bad.

5. **Karma teaches us spirituality.** The purpose of living in spiritual awareness is to create an Earth where we will rediscover our oneness, our common humanity. All of us need to thrive and be respected for who or what we are. Earth is a place where we can learn to respect the similarities and the differences between ourselves and our planet and live in loving tolerance of those differences. Great beauty, wisdom, and opportunity are within all who are living a life in consciousness and awareness.

6. **Karma teaches us to live in peace.** Positive and negative karma refers to actual positive or negative actions. It also refers to an intent or motive. For example, even if we do the smallest daily action or deed with great love in our hearts, we can change our life from one of constantly creating negative karma to one of constantly creating good karma. Mother Teresa said, "If we have no peace, it is because we have forgotten that we belong to each other." It is important to live our lives in peace and harmony in order to complete our spiritual evolution.

7. **Karma teaches us conscious awareness.** Every thought that we have and every word that we speak either adds to or takes away from the light of humanity. Everything that we think and say about ourselves, whether it is silently to ourselves or aloud to others, either adds to or takes away from the light of humanity. Everything that we think and say to and about others, whether it is silently to ourselves or aloud to others, either adds to or takes away from the light of humanity. There are no insignificant thoughts or words; each one has energy and an effect. Living our lives in

conscious awareness helps us to live in the light and be one with the Divine or Creator.

8. Karma teaches us to live our lives with love.
We should live our lives in love of others and for others without any expectation of repayment. We should live our lives in love, forgiving hurts against us, asking for the consolation of dead relatives and friends, and loving everyone with no distinction between friend and foe. This brings about true lasting joy and happiness, good karma, and virtue to ourselves, our loved ones, and the world. If we are kind to others, even those who are not kind to us, we will find true happiness. This begins by living our lives with love.

9. All karmic debts must be paid in full.
A karmic debt is a debt that we have accumulated either in this life or in a past life. It is typically the result of something that occurred between someone else and ourselves or from an interaction between our planet and ourselves. All karmic debts must be paid either in our present life or in a future life. An example of a karmic debt may be someone who dedicated a career to cutting down trees or something else that harmed the environment in one of his/her past lives. This individual would then have to balance and pay this karmic debt by having a career or volunteering in a field or profession that involved healing or helping the environment or planet in some way.

10. Karma lives in the law of cause and effect.
The law of cause and effect basically states that for every movement of energy that takes the form of an image, feeling, desire, belief, expectation, or action, there is a corresponding effect. For this reason, the law of cause and effect influences every aspect of our karma. In order to make the most of the law of cause

and effect, we must live consciously and recognize that we are the creator of our own reality. The goal of karma is to ensure that we link our actions (the cause) with their results (the effect).

11. **Great karmic strides can be made with intention.** Intention is the most important of all mental processes because it guides the mind in determining how to engage with virtuous, non-virtuous, or neutral objects. Just as iron is powerlessly drawn to a magnet, our minds are drawn to the object of our intentions. An intention is a mental thought or action that may be expressed through either a physical or a verbal action. With intention, what we dwell on, we create.

12. **Karma cultivates knowledge, wisdom, and compassion.** As we learn our spiritual lessons and karmic actions through the processes of reincarnation and karma, we will grow and cultivate our gardens of knowledge, wisdom, and compassion. Though karma often does not appear merciful to us, it is the most compassionate and effective way to restore balance and teach our souls our spiritual lessons. We have all made mistakes because we have not always followed the highest voice from within, thus causing suffering to others and ultimately to ourselves. The voice of conscience within each of us lets us see the possible results of the right and wrong actions we choose in life. We have knowledge to interpret these actions and the wisdom, compassion, and free will to make choices in our lives using this wisdom and compassion throughout each life we live.

Basically, it is the Law of Love which governs our nature. Without this, the universe would not exist. The Law of Love states, "You shall love your neighbor as yourself." Who is your neighbor? Everyone is your neighbor. The Law of Love really means "Love all people as yourself" because everyone is us, and we are everyone. The Law of Love is put into action by The Golden Rule. If we love other people as ourselves, then how should we treat them? We should treat them exactly as we would like to be treated. The Golden Rule states, "Treat others as you would like to be treated." All karma can be dissolved in love or by the Law of Love. There is no reason why we should ever fight, no matter what the cause might be. Love is always the answer and all that there is.

The best method for resolving karma is service. Service is a good way to eliminate all bad karma and create good karma in its place. The process is something like this: as we serve, we draw energy to ourselves. By giving energy, we get energy.

Any act of service is a deposit into the universal karmic bank. Whenever we are busy serving the needs of someone else, we are creating good karma. This service will influence our own karma, as well as that of the people we serve. By such action, we allow them greater peace of mind in order to promote balance in their own lives. So the law itself sets in motion its own fulfillment. As we serve, we demonstrate love. As we demonstrate love, by karmic law we get love. Learning to live in accordance with the spiritual rules of eternal life, we will help improve the quality of our lives.

Karma can be changed during the course of a life. If we live in consciousness and are aware of karma, we can strive to change events in our lives. Our energy and our aura is a result of words, actions, and thoughts. By being positive, giving service to our Earth and all things on it, and by being grateful, we will be able to change our energy and, therefore, our karma.

It is important to realize that fate is always in our own hands. There is an old Buddhist parable that goes something like this:

In a time long past, there was an old monk who through diligent practice had attained a certain degree of spiritual penetration. He had a young novice who was about eight years old. One day the monk looked at the boy's face and saw that he would die within the next few months. Saddened by this, he told the boy to take a long holiday and go and visit his parents.

"Take your time," said the monk. "Don't hurry back," for he felt the boy should be with his family when he died.

Three months later, to his astonishment, the monk saw the boy walking back up the mountain. When he arrived, he looked intently at his face and saw that the boy would now live to a ripe old age.

"Tell me everything that happened while you were away," said the monk.

So the boy started to tell of his journey down from the mountain. He told of villages and towns he passed through, of rivers forded and mountains climbed. Then he told how one day he came upon a stream that was flooding. He noticed, as he tried to pick his way across the flowing stream, that a colony of ants had become trapped on a small island formed by the flooding stream. Moved by compassion for these poor creatures, he took a branch off a tree and laid it across one flow of the stream until it touched the little island. As the ants made their way across, the boy held the branch steady until he was sure all the ants had escaped to dry land. Then he went on his way.

"So," thought the old monk to himself, "that is why the gods have lengthened his days."

We can begin at this moment to live a happier, richer life, one that adds a vast amount to our karmic bank account. We can work toward greater balance in all areas of our lives, including health, sex, money, and influence. We will return to learn a few more lessons, search for more truth, do as much as we can for others, and move a little closer toward spiritual perfection. We will finish this life, leave for awhile, return, pick up our karmic bank book, and continue on our journey in pursuit of our spiritual lessons and balance. As incredible as it may seem, in time all karmic debts will be paid, all earthly lives will be lived, total enlightenment will be achieved, and self-mastery will be attained.

Chapter 4

Healing & Evolving Through Spirit

At any moment, you have a choice that either leads you closer to your spirit or further away from it.

~Thich Nhat Hanh

*I*t's hard to conceive that before we were born we picked our lives for our own spiritual evolution and advancement. Why would we want to spend a life suffering in Africa, live a life dying from AIDS, or have a child that passes on from cancer? These questions are hard to answer, but the answer is that we pick our lives for our spiritual growth and evolution. In most cases, we are usually blocked from remembering so we can make these advancements. Healing and evolving through spirit awakens our souls and uplifts our consciousness so we can make huge advancements in our spiritual evolution.

Not everyone can feel happy or contented, but everyone does feel pain, and this is what connects us to humanity. There is an old saying that "the wounded healer heals." The more pain and suffering we have in our lives, the more we can connect to humanity and the concept of oneness, the more we have a chance to heal and to help others heal through our own pain and suffering. If we have a child who dies of cancer, we can certainly connect quickly with other parents in the same situation and even offer help, advice, support, and a shoulder to cry on. This pain connects us to many other people in the same situation and gives us an opportunity to help humanity and grow with our spiritual lessons.

Some of us grew up living a hard life. Growing up poor is certainly no easy task when we constantly hear our parents fighting or screaming about money. Some of us have had absentee parents or emotionally and or physically abusive parents. This is tough, but when we live to heal and evolve through spirit, through our awareness we can end up thanking our parents for connecting us to humanity. Without pain, most of us wouldn't learn about dimensional consciousness and how to grow peace from a quiet place within our souls. Saying "I'm sorry" or "I forgive you" is not easy. There are always spiritual lessons in our lives, and, in most cases, we are unable to move on or remove obstacles from our paths until these lessons are learned.

Sometimes it is hard to forgive our parents, family members, friends, or loved ones and move on. We tend to blame others for everything going wrong in our lives, but deep down it is important that we take responsibility for ourselves on every level of our being, including our thoughts, words, and actions. It is never too late to pick up the pieces, move on, and, more importantly, be happy. Being able to forgive is hard to do. It takes incredible strength, a courageous spirit, and great inner love, but the simple act of forgiveness can create great healing within our souls.

There is no real road map or recipe for us to follow when we are learning to heal through spirit. What is important is for us to pull back from our situations and look at our bigger picture. Asking, "Why am I here, what is my life's purpose, and how can I contribute to humanity?" is a good place to start. Pulling back and trying to grasp the meaning of some of our life's lessons will help us understand why we are in our current situation. Often these lessons mean healing and evolving through our spiritual growth and advancement. When we learn our spiritual lessons quickly, we often move on to a better place at a faster pace. If we don't learn our lessons, we will have repeating cycles over and over in the same or similar situations until they are learned.

If we look at the universe as a large tapestry with us as a single thread weaving in and out of other threads, we can see a bigger picture of what is happening in our lives. If we have no challenges or strife in life, we wouldn't have multiple opportunities for spiritual growth and evolvement presented to us, and then what would all this be for?

There are times in life when we have all felt abandoned and alone—as if there was no one around to help us move through troubled times. Our experiences have shown that this is not true because we have so bravely taken on difficult or challenging situations for our spiritual lessons and have done so with grace and compassion. We don't have to advertise or tell others of the awareness we have gained. Just by being who we are, we embody the collective experiences of life and all the wisdom we have achieved. These vibrational frequencies are then picked up and felt by others because our awareness and vibrations will affect those around us by the principle of *like vibrations*. That is, if we hold a certain vibrational frequency, energy, knowledge, and awareness, eventually those around us will also begin to embody some of that energy. With the principle of *like vibrations*, people with similar energies will also be attracted to us, and those without a similar vibrational frequency will be repelled.

We can have a powerful effect on humanity just by living the life that we have chosen and by going through hard times, spiritual lessons, and experiences with love and compassion in our hearts. This is what healing and evolving through spirit is about—finding and acknowledging the great gifts we have within our souls. Although life isn't always easy in a human body, our higher self or spirit knows that through our lives, we are able to help others who also face difficult times. By finding the gifts that have come to us as a result of our consciousness and awareness and sharing these gifts and realizations with others, our own life's purpose can unfold.

We are able to fulfill our *purpose* just by being the radiant souls that we are. There is no way that we cannot be who we are as a soul, and so our *purpose* is unfolding with every breath that we take. We are a part of the living web of life here on Earth, and each soul within that web is a part of the whole, unique, and divine plan for all of humanity.

When discovering who we are as souls, a new freedom emerges from within our hearts. This freedom is the freedom of the soul, the freedom of love, and the freedom to be and live with all the beauty and grace within because this is who we truly are. Our angels and guides are always with us during our journey. They are always within our touch, sight, and hearing as they offer gentle reminders of who we are, why we're here, and how to find our way in this crazy life on Earth. When healing through Spirit, we must have faith in our choices, in our hearts, and in love, for we are always on the right path. We are always loved and never alone.

Being on the right path is remembering the power of forgiveness because forgiveness is important when dealing with old emotions that can be carried around within our hearts. These lower vibrational energies may block or slow our own abilities to deal with life's day-to-day issues in positive and constructive ways. Forgiveness allows us to release old pain and open our spirit for newer, higher vibrational energy. It also allows us to feel neutral on controversial issues so that our soul can advance to new, more interesting or important spiritual lessons.

Dealing with a loved one who is suffering from addiction, anger, or fear can definitely cause us to stuff our emotions down while we are trying to cope with the issues at hand. Suppressing emotions out of love for another can cause us to feel resentment toward the individual who is addicted or acting out in anger/fear and toward ourselves for getting into the situation. Forgiveness can work both ways by truly forgiving and releasing the other person or even ourselves from the expectations of being perfect.

For our spirits, it is important that we step forward in our lives no matter the circumstances, clear our emotional bodies or auras, and free some space in our hearts to work on spiritual issues. Working on spiritual issues will always help us make advances in our spiritual evolution.

If we think of our emotional body or auric field like a computer hard drive, there is only so much memory it can hold. Then it starts to freeze up when running old programs. That is where many of us are today—with so many old programs running in our emotional and spiritual bodies from old and hurtful memories from the past sometimes even from past lives. This leaves no room for new programs to run or to even be installed, so they are pushed away. Procrastination happens when we are spiritually or emotionally overloaded. It is important for us to delete old programs in our spiritual and emotional hard drives to allow space for newer and better programs to be installed.

Great opportunities lie within us, even deep beneath old scars and betrayals. There is much energy in our Spirits that can be tied up and wasted on old feelings and emotions. Even though we have worked hard on releasing these old patterns and fears, they can still affect us. Remember that all of these old patterns are just karmic checks, balances, and spiritual lessons being played out. Living a life in awareness and consciousness, embracing these situations for what they are, and learning to grow from them will always help us with these lessons.

Forgiveness is the foundation of all spiritual work and growth because it is by living in awareness of forgiveness that we can truly know our own life's journey and purpose. Forgiveness is not a process of giving something to another person who may not deserve anything in return. It is a process of turning our energy inward and using the power of love to look at relationships within ourselves and others.

When we are anchored in forgiveness, we are within the spiritual realm rather than in the realm of emotions or the mind. How often do we forgive others while still holding on to that corner of our heart that pouts, "I am right and they are wrong, but I forgive them"?

These thoughts come from the mind and the emotions and not from spirit. It is difficult for us to release anger, remorse, guilt, or resentment through the mind, rational thinking, or logical reasons of why we should forgive. The only reason that it is logical to forgive another is because holding onto negative energy hinders the flow of love into our own lives and blocks our spiritual balance and peace. Recognizing this pushes our minds to wrap around this concept and allow forgiveness to come from great depths within our souls. Love is always the energy that gives and maintains life. By forgiving others, even those who seem not to deserve it, we can bring life-giving energy into our bodies. Then it becomes easier to make the choice to forgive.

Any time we are experiencing apathy, lethargy, exhaustion, confusion, or a sense of being overwhelmed, we may have old cobwebs about forgiveness hanging around the corners of our hearts that need to be released. When anchoring our hearts in forgiveness, we can release these issues to our guides, angels, or the universe and trust that our hearts will heal.

Love is the healing energy that binds all of humanity. The issues that seem to defy forgiveness are always about love: love that we never received, love offered but rejected or betrayed, or love used as manipulation or control. There are many ways in which our issues are tied to love. By tying up our spiritual energy reserves into old issues, we are limiting the vibrational level of love available in our present lives. Now is the time to begin searching our hearts to find out how to truly forgive.

We are emerging into a time of great clarity and direct purpose on our paths during this point in our spiritual evolution. We cannot be shadowed by yesterday's old and outdated energies and must remain clear and alive in our current or present moment. We need to ask to accept each day anew without any burdens of previous troubles or hurts. Each evening and morning, we should review any old emotions or hurts from the day before that have been carried around and work through them, letting them go, and allowing our spiritual light to shine through.

All of us have old energy tied up in our auras and in our hearts that creates challenges and blockages in our lives. We are all in a process of learning how to clear these issues, entities, thought forms, fears, and old wounds from our bodies so that we can all ascend into higher dimensional consciousness and become the enlightened beings that we are.

Many of the great spiritual lessons that our experiences teach us are not recognized while we are in the midst of these lessons. Only later do we see the profound teachings these experiences offered us. These lessons can help us immensely when future strife and loss enter our lives. They will not eliminate the pain, but they can give us greater strength, deeper hope, and clearer understanding in our lives. They can also give us courage to stay in the turmoil and to trust that we will survive our struggles and not be destroyed by them. Instead, we will learn and draw strength from them.

We don't know others' spiritual lessons or their spiritual evolutionary paths, so we must never judge anyone because it lowers our vibrational frequency and leaves us without compassion. Keeping compassion in our hearts for all living and non-living things is important since compassion is yet another powerful emotion that heals us all.

One of the hardest things to do in life is to let go of the past. Dwelling on issues for too long can close our heart chakras and keep us from being fully present in our current moment. When we are not fully present in the now, we are not living our lives to the fullest, we are not free, and our energy fields get tied up running old programs, blocking us from receiving love and knowledge from the universe.

Our decision to embark on a path of self discovery, self-healing, and spiritual growth is one that requires great courage, perseverance, and determination. There is a truth to our purpose, and this truth always lies within our heart chakras. Often we have forgotten about opening our heart chakras to receive guidance from our angels, guides, and the universe itself. Sometimes we hold onto frightening secrets and hide our largest demons within our hearts. These hurtful memories can lie buried deep within because we have the intent to never uncover and deal with these emotions. The mark of great warriors or masters is that they are willing time and again to face their own darkness, their own demons, and to have the courage to face their inner selves. This requires stripping down the layers that have built up on false foundations with which hurts have been covered.

These layers unbalance our lives and distort our true potential and progression. The process of stripping away whatever fails to serve us in a positive manner requires great courage and knowledge. To be whole, we must live in the truth of our purpose. When we feel our energy being tied up with old destructive programs, we must face the truth and deal with the issues at hand, or the same issues will appear in our current life as well as lifetimes to come.

My heart cries out for the souls in spiritual pain, for they only need the tiniest spark of love to begin the process of spiritual self-healing. Many souls do not understand this, nor do they realize how much spiritual pain they are in. The energy is changing and has been changing on Earth for the better. We should take advantage of this opportunity to lay emotional pain to rest once and for all. The universe is offering to reach out and heal us, so spiritual growth can take us to new heights, new energies, and higher vibrational frequencies. The chance is now, and we only need to open our hearts to reach for it.

When embarking on a course of healing, we should walk with both our eyes and our hearts open. There will be many who will be here to help and support us on both the physical and spiritual planes along our path. Part of our healing process is discovering our inner truth and realizing help surrounds us and is with us at every moment during this process in our lives.

The issues and realizations that surface during our healing process can be incredibly painful. This can often make us feel angry and resentful and project these feelings onto others.

Some of us will not want to accept new energy into our lives and will turn change into drama in order to create diversions that prevent us from examining underlying issues. When we do this, we refuse to truly look within ourselves and face what is there, that is the gifts of growth, of learning our lessons, of spiritual advancement. When committing to our own healing and growth, we must listen with our ears and our hearts as we absorb all that we are given in life, both good and bad.

We should always question ourselves, our lives, and our motives. When we seek the truth both within and outside ourselves, we can help others be mindful to do the same. As mentioned earlier, souls will attract the energy of other souls who have similar life lessons. By looking at our friends or family, we can also reflect on what life lessons we need to work on. This is because in any healthy relationship that is devoted to growth and spiritual development, there is always a give and take of energy among family and friends. We are all at different levels of growth and spiritual development. Others in our life may not be able to understand lessons in the way we do because they are not yet capable of that level of understanding. Often we must walk away from these relationships for our own sake, or these people may block and drain our vital energy. When our energies no longer match either friends or family members, we need to move on to others who do match our vibrational frequency. There is nothing sad about this process. It is all about understanding our spiritual growth process.

Through courage, perseverance, and love for self, we can make the commitment to heal and evolve through our spirit and help others to do the same with theirs.

Chapter 5

Spiritual Development and the Heart and Soul Connection

Every thought, action, decision, or feeling creates an eddy in the interlocking, interbalancing, ever-moving energy fields of life, leaving a permanent record for all time. This realization can be intimidating when it first dawns on us, but it becomes a springboard for rapid evolution.

~David Hawkins

We often ask ourselves why are we here on this planet? What is the reason for all our experiences, both good and bad? We do have a purpose that we planned before we were born. We agreed to all our experiences before our feet hit this Earth. It is incredibly tough to imagine that we agreed to be raped, have our children die of cancer, spend our lives crippled, or endure other challenging events that occur in our lives.

Why in the world would we agree to such experiences? What possible good could come of such pain? These questions are hard to answer, but the answer is that we experience these situations for our spiritual growth and development, for others' spiritual growth and development, to play out our soul's karma, and to achieve our spiritual mastery.

Not everyone in the world experiences emotions like joy, laughter, gratitude, and other happy emotions, but everyone does experience pain. Pain is what ties us all together and connects us to humanity. We are all one and when someone is suffering in Asia, Africa, or America, we are all suffering because we are all threads on the same tapestry. Our experiences, both good and bad, should not be feared. There is nothing to fear in life, not even death, as there is no such thing. Whatever situations we came to learn and grow from, it is important for our soul's development and our spiritual evolution, so no experience in our life is ever in vain.

Due to our spiritual development, we will come back over and over until we learn the lessons our soul has chosen to learn. Some of these lessons are quite simple, such as learning not to be envious or learning how to give. Other lessons may seem simple, but they are not. It could take us fifty lifetimes to learn one lesson if we are not aware of why we are here and do not recognize lessons we need to learn while they are occurring.

It is important not to waste a life by not knowing what our life's purpose is or how we can contribute to humanity. We must find these things out early in life so we can all work on the spiritual issues we are here to work on.

Sometimes we can find ourselves in difficult situations. We may be going through a divorce, hate our boss, have a child with a terminal disease, or be struggling financially. There are lessons for our soul in each and every one of these situations. We create our own realities so if we don't like the situations we're in, we can try to learn our spiritual lessons, raise our vibrational frequency, and get ourselves out of any repeating cycles we may be in.

Many handicapped people believe that if it were not for a genetic mistake or being a victim of an accidental injury that damaged their bodies, their lives would be more fulfilled. As souls, we choose our bodies and our circumstances for a reason. Living in a body that demands extra care and attention does not necessarily have to involve karmic debt because of past life responsibility for an injury to someone else. When a soul is inside a challenged body, this choice can involve a learning path to another type of lesson and can also involve great spiritual advancement.

It is difficult to tell a newly-injured person trying to cope with a physical disability that there is a chance to spiritually advance more quickly than others that have healthy bodies or minds. Often this knowledge must come through self-discovery by living in awareness of our higher purpose. Many members of our culture discriminate against people who are physically or mentally challenged, which creates a heavy burden for those with disabilities. Overcoming the obstacles of physical ailments and pain makes our soul stronger for the ordeal. Our bodies are an important part of the lessons we set for ourselves in each life that we live, for there can be powerful spiritual lessons in discovering the strength of spirit that lies within ourselves. Being strong does not necessarily imply a powerful body or great intellect; great strength implies the power we have within our spirits.

From lifetime to lifetime, we may choose a life where we are a strong man and another life where we are a physically challenged woman. A strong man may have lessons about experiencing all of the senses of the physical body to the fullest and nothing more. We may also choose the body of a physically challenged woman to gain intellectual concentration. A broken body may lead a soul to read and study more, making the mind an important tool in that lifetime. In both of these scenarios, a soul may find that our strength actually comes from within and not from our physical bodies. There are any number of scenarios and lessons that we consider before choosing our bodies.

We can also search for self-expression by developing various aspects of our character. If a soul chooses a life of extreme circumstances, down the line this will be counterbalanced by an opposite choice to even out all experiences for we cannot have one without the other. For example, we may choose a life with great wealth and another life in complete poverty. By experiencing and surviving all these challenges, our soul is strengthened, great spiritual lessons are learned, and advancement in our spiritual evolution can take place.

There is a poignant and beautiful connection between our heart and our soul. All our experiences in life can affect both our heart and, therefore, our soul's spiritual growth. We all decided before we came to Earth that we would embody specific energies and situations that humanity is struggling with at this time. Most of us are finding our way through our lives by shifting and transmuting these experiences into positive circumstances and therefore, positive karma.

It is truly the healers of the world who choose the most difficult of paths, and this is a gift to humanity. It is a gift because often healers or teachers will take on additional hardships and will transmute this energy to more positive circumstances. By doing this, they can show us the way to shift our own energy with similar situations. They take on these hardships and shift them in order to spiritually share the burden that humanity carries. In a way, we are all healers in this world. We may ask, "How am I supposed to be a healer when my own life is so difficult?" By sharing our experiences with others, change can be made on a global level. For example, Betty Ford was an alcoholic that learned the process of recovery and healing. She then opened clinics to teach and help others to recover and heal.

The connection between our heart and soul lies in the fact that we pick our lives before we are born. Things we feel in our heart come from our soul's lessons that we want to learn here on Earth at this time. It comes from past karmic experiences we wish to balance. In most cases, we are not able to remember previous lives or lessons but can stay aware of current life issues and lessons, and this is where our spiritual growth can be made—in our current moment.

Our angels and guides work hard behind the scenes to create specific experiences that will help us with our spiritual growth and our spiritual evolution. Karmic opportunities are created without our knowledge or pitfalls we experienced in former lives. It is difficult to have great spiritual growth and spiritual evolution if we remember our experiences from all the lives that we have previously lived because, most likely, we would tend to avoid karmic situations if we had knowledge of them. Engaging in self-discovery is our best route to wisdom in each life.

We are not human beings on a spiritual journey but, in fact, spiritual beings on a human journey. For our soul, coming to Earth is like traveling away from our home to a foreign land. Some things seem familiar, but most seem strange until we have a chance to get used to them, especially unforgiving conditions found on this tough playground we call Earth. Our home on the spiritual plane is a place of absolute peace, total acceptance, and complete love where we are able to instantly manifest anything and everything we want or need at any given moment. As our souls leave the spiritual realm, we no longer have easy access to these unique gifts and this can be a tough adjustment.

While on Earth, we must learn to cope with intolerance, anger, and sadness while searching for joy and love. Along the way we must not lose our integrity, sacrifice goodness for survival, or acquire superior or inferior attitudes to those around us. We know that living in an imperfect world will help us to appreciate the true meaning of perfection. Before incarnating back on Earth, we ask for courage and humility on our journey into a new life. While we are growing awareness on Earth, the quality of our existence will also grow through our karmic balance sheet. This is how we are tested. Passing this test is our goal to achieve our spiritual awakening, ascension, spiritual growth, and spiritual evolution.

Our souls are connected to our hearts in each life that we live. What our souls have experienced in previous lifetimes can be brought forth into our current lives. Often these are lessons that were not learned in previous lives, which will come forth to our current life so we can try to learn them again. These lessons may be more difficult for some and easier for others. If we are aware of our purpose here, our lives will be less challenging. If we live our lives without consciousness and awareness, it can be more difficult.

We choose to come to Earth for spiritual lessons as opposed to going to other planets because Earth holds many special attributes and qualities not found in other parts of the universe. It is known to be a particularly tough playground but also holds experiences, such as bravery and great emotions that are not found in other worlds. Souls that achieve all their spiritual lessons from incarnating here have incredible insight, great depth, and exceptional wisdom as compared to souls that have incarnated in other universes. It may take 800 life times to reach these goals but reach them we will. Earth can be a cruel world but also a place where incredible spiritual strides can be made.

For example, a soul named Marta spent many lifetimes incarnating in other worlds and chose to come to Earth to help excel in her spiritual growth process. Marta selected a life in India as a woman who had lost her children. In order to receive the full impact of a disruptive planet, Marta was the poorest of poor and lived in absolute squalor. A brave choice indeed for a soul who never incarnated on such a tough planet.

During her life in India, Marta had many challenging experiences. A childless family took Marta's daughter from her by paying the owner of her shelter where she lived. Marta spent the rest of her life struggling with the cruelties found on our planet.

Marta chose this particularly difficult life because she wanted to be in a strenuous physical world that produces vigorous and insightful souls. Her experiences, as horrific and painful as they were, made Marta a better teacher in the spiritual realm. Marta's spiritual lessons were about overcoming loss and discovering great inner strength. In her grief, she found the incredible power of her spirit.

Marta's soul chose a hard life that affected her heart in the most profound of ways. Her experiences and opportunities for spiritual growth were incredible. It was a hard and painful life full of sadness and anger, but the lessons extracted from this brave soul's decision to live this difficult life will stay with her in all her future lives. The wisdom gained from such a difficult life will lead to better understanding and awareness in each and every life that she lives.

When Marta completes her work on Earth, she will be strengthened in ways beyond what other souls could if not incarnated here on our Earth but in other universes. She will be a more effective teacher and leader from what she has experienced.

It is foolish to believe that our souls have not lived challenging lives, such as Marta. We will live every life scenario that is necessary to balance our spiritual growth. If we live a life of wealth without giving to the poor, we may have to live a life of poverty to understand how important it is to be in service to humanity.

When we channel our physical, emotional, and mental energy into soulful pursuits, we create a meaningful life—one filled with a sense of purpose, vitality, and aliveness that characterize our true meaning for being here.

In the end, it doesn't really matter what brings us to remember who we are or why we're here. The connection between our heart and soul is a strong one, for our soul seeks lessons of the heart in each and every moment that we live.

When we make the connection between our heart and soul, it is easy to see that if someone loves, we all feel love. If someone gives, we all give. If someone is hurting, we all feel hurt. It is the Law of One.

Each of us is blessed with unique lessons and special gifts in life that can be used to help make the world a kinder, more loving, just, and beautiful world in which to live. The heart and soul connection teaches us that we can and must unite our hearts and souls in pursuit of these noble lessons.

Chapter 6
Spiritual Lessons in a Spiritual Evolution

We count our miseries carefully and accept our blessings without much thought.

~Mother Theresa

Spiritualism represents our inner soul to ourselves, and through spiritualism, our spirit guides us as we walk our path here on Earth. We all need spiritual nourishment to guide and direct us throughout our lives so we can learn our spiritual lessons and progress during our time here on Earth towards our spiritual evolution.

Being a spiritual person means living by The Golden Rule, "Do unto others as you would have them do unto you." Everyday life allows us to express ourselves in a positive way to enlighten our paths with goodness, raise our vibrational frequency, and live within higher levels of consciousness.

To implement the teaching of spirituality is to utilize principles where we practice what we preach and live without judgment. We don't know what someone else's life purpose is or what spiritual lessons have been planned for other people. Practicing spiritual understanding and love for others is a good platform on which to stand during our soul's lifetime. Living a life with grace, compassion, kindness, and love aids us in our spiritual evolution.

Seeking spiritual guidance is a good way for us to understand our spiritual lessons in our spiritual evolution. This understanding will bring about a heightened consciousness and awareness needed during this time of ascension and great energy shifts on Earth. We have come to the time in our spiritual evolution where we must reach within to understand who we are and the reason for our being.

Seeking spiritual lessons in a spiritual evolution will lead us to a level of understanding that is needed at this time so we can learn our lessons and ascend into higher dimensional consciousness. Today we are experiencing many spiritual lessons and acquiring greater spiritual awareness in our day-to-day lives.

We often wonder why we are here—what's the purpose and meaning of our everyday lives? Our soul agreed to specific lessons in each life that we live, and these lessons will be experienced during our time here on Earth. Sometimes we are not able to learn or achieve all our spiritual lessons and will need to come back again and try to finish them in another lifetime. If a particular spiritual lesson is not learned, our angels and guides will work tirelessly behind the scenes to give us as many chances as possible to learn this lesson under different circumstances. The variables can change with each lifetime when specific circumstances or layouts are not allowing us to learn our spiritual lessons in these various scenarios. If we don't pass a grade in school, we have to repeat that grade again, and spiritual lessons are the same way. Whatever lessons we don't master in a particular life will have to be repeated by coming back and trying again. Depending on our guides, planning committee, and our own free-will decisions, the experiences for our lessons can be made easier or more difficult the next time around. Either way, the lessons will continue until they are completed.

We are here on Earth studying different subjects and learning different lessons as we do in school, except we are learning various spiritual lessons to earn a passing grade, so to speak. Each lifetime's growth, experiences, and karma are brought forth to our next life and can and will help us with our lessons. During each lifetime, our soul gains more and more knowledge until we have mastered our lessons and can progress to the next level. In the end, our spiritual mastery will always be our goal.

We are all here experiencing spiritual growth whether we are aware of it or not. If we meditate and place our mind, heart, and soul together, then our spiritual lessons and the purpose of our spiritual evolution may be acquired more easily. Once we understand our spiritual purpose, wisdom from above can flow through us and help us fulfill our life's purpose here on Earth.

We are all sitting on a spiritual gold mine, filled with enriched experiences that can make life much happier and meaningful if we are more aware and conscious of these experiences. We note some of our spiritual experiences in our lives, but many more are missed. This is why many of our life's lessons are lost—because we lack awareness. This is also why so many of us find ourselves going around in circles without understanding why our lives are the way they are. We need to look for patterns in our lives. We must rise above and look down at ourselves. If we see what is happening from an elevated and objective standpoint, we can ask ourselves, "What is my lesson here? How can I learn and grow from this situation or this experience?" Within each and every day of our lives, we have an opportunity to grow from these experiences. Spiritual lessons and guidance can quite simply come from a song on the radio while we are driving our cars as most of our lessons are not overly complicated. We should look for any and every opportunity to increase our consciousness and awareness with this realization of how easy some of our lessons can be.

As spiritual lessons are usually quite simple and are frequently about love and forgiveness, it is important to anchor love in our hearts while learning our lessons. Watching for patterns and looking for the spiritual lessons our soul agreed to

57

experience becomes easier when we anchor our hearts in love. Once we figure out what the lessons are, we will be able to move out of our old patterns and on to new experiences. As we all move forward, our lessons will become easier for us, but we must be living in awareness so we can recognize and grow from these opportunities.

With each life, our soul may be working on as little as one or as many as twenty lessons at any given time. There is no limit to how many issues we can work on in any given lifetime—it is up to us. In retrospect, our lessons may seem quite simple, but while we are working on them, it may seem impossible to figure out why specific circumstances or situations are occurring over and over in our lives. If we have spiritual lessons about forgiveness, this topic will recur with people we know and love, or even complete strangers, until we tackle and master these lessons. We might find ourselves asking, "Why does this keep happening in my life?" The answer may come by our writing down or keeping a journal of cycles or patterns in our life, so we may better identify our spiritual lessons. In addition, if we keep our heart chakras open at all times, our angels and guides will be able to come into our hearts and help us conquer the lessons we are here to learn, no matter how easy or difficult they may seem.

Discovering spiritual lessons as they unfold from circumstances in our lives is a skill that grows with awareness and practice. This skill can be developed through the use of a variety of spiritual exercises or a wide range of activities that can help broaden our spiritual awareness. There are different types of spiritual exercises because all of us have different states of awareness, and the only way we can discover if one particular exercise will work is to try it out. Some may not work to our satisfaction the first time, so practicing a technique several times before discarding it is always a good way for us to develop specific or unique abilities. There are a variety of spiritual exercises to choose from that are in tune with our present state of consciousness.

Consider the following techniques to help you determine your spiritual lessons:

1. Find peace within.

What makes you peaceful? What obstacles in life have either blocked your peace or, on the other hand, brought you to peace? Remember, peace starts from within, so it is important to keep this emotion in our heart at all times when determining a spiritual lesson.

2. Cultivate compassion.

Are you living your life with compassion? As human beings we all have the potential to be either happy and compassionate people or miserable and harmful to others. The Dalai Lama says, "Thus we can strive gradually to become more compassionate, that is, we can develop both genuine sympathy for others' suffering and the will to help remove their pain. As a result, our own serenity and inner strength will increase." Thus, it is when we reach out to others who are suffering in some way, we are practicing compassion and following the Dali Lama's advice while simultaneously finding greater peace within our own lives.

3. Live consciously.

You are made of energy composed of your thoughts, words, actions, feelings, a physical element, and spirit. You can live consciously to create illumination, joy, healing, hope, balance, harmony, courage, strength, love, wisdom, and power from within your soul and your spirit by being aware of your every thought and action and its effect on all that is.

4. Remember your soul's purpose.

Your physical body is a temporary vessel where you choose to house your soul for a short span of time in the realms of material expression. Because of this, your soul has a record of all that it has experienced throughout many ages and lifetimes called the Akashic Records. Accessing these records through meditation can help us remember the lessons we are working on and our soul's purpose.

By finding our inner peace, cultivating our compassion, and living consciously, we can remember our soul's purpose. Staying balanced and in harmony during our lives and remembering that we are here on this tough playground for a reason will help us get through difficult times.

By developing techniques to help us with our spiritual lessons, we can then strive for spiritual awareness and consciousness. Spiritual awareness and consciousness is the process by which we begin to explore our own being in order to become whole and reunite our spirits with our physical bodies in a commonality of purpose.

Since life on Earth is a school for us as developing souls, spiritual lessons within our spiritual evolution are embedded in our daily experiences of life. Looking for spiritual light is part of our purpose as a soul living on Earth at this time. This is our playground for living our lessons, loving one another, learning all that we can, and most importantly, having fun.

There are numerous experiences that can open our eyes and hearts to specific aspects of our lives that will allow wisdom and love to lead us in our spiritual growth and development. The biggest obstacle to our spiritual growth is thinking that we already know the answers in life or being unaware of why we are really here.

As we grow spiritually stronger with each life that we live, our goal is to be able to take any and all incidents from life and examine them from the viewpoint of our soul learning a lesson. Spiritual *growth* is that which is important in each life that we live. Through spiritual growth we learn how to live life more responsibly with greater wisdom and love.

So often, people who fail say, "I simply can't deal with my life. Everything is wrong, and I can't get over this problem." When we are feeling down, at odds with people, and we don't have the confidence needed in life, it's a good idea to sit down and write out what difficulties we may experiencing and what lessons we may learn from them. Writing down these difficulties can allow us to see our spiritual lessons in their true light, which will give us means to obtain feedback about the spiritual quality of our relationships, our own true spirituality, as well as our own spiritual development or the development of surrounding loved ones.

For example, if we have a father who is an alcoholic, we can look at our spiritual lessons in this way: Recognize his *failures* as strength-building spiritual lessons for the entire family. Alcoholics can teach great lessons in the art of forgiveness and caring. Giving and suffering can be gifts because we can better understand what it is like to give and still love someone even though they have wronged us. An alcoholic may give the gift of humility so that we might know compassion. An alcoholic may give into weaknesses so that we might know strength. It is sacrifice on the part of the alcoholic to teach a family the forgiving, compassionate, and kind ways that we all share but have forgotten to some degree. We may also discover great inner strength to walk away if the alcoholic is abusive. There are any number of spiritual lessons to be learned in this one experience.

There are any number of lessons to be learned and many aspects of each lesson to take note of. Sometimes it is a painful journey that propels us forward, and we experience these situations to help us grow as a developing soul. By learning and becoming aware of our spiritual lessons, we can find out how to heal and how to progress with our spiritual purpose. What is our spiritual purpose? The spiritual purpose of all life experience is the spiritual intent of an expanding awareness and consciousness.

There is a compass of sorts that can help direct and guide us in our lives, and it is called the Golden Compass of Spiritual Lessons. By following eight short guidelines, we can all make sure we spiritually evolve with each life that we live.

The Golden Compass of Spiritual Lessons

1. Live life in forgiveness.

Forgiveness is living in a state of grace, and we are only truly happy when we forgive everyone in our lives. Living in forgiveness is one of the most difficult spiritual lessons because it requires tremendous amounts of strength. It takes a lot of energy to hold onto hatred or disrespect to others but when we live in forgiveness, we can affect our karma in a positive way by being in the light of all of human consciousness.

2. Love is all we need.

By keeping love in our hearts at all times, it will make it easier to change our energy or vibrational frequency because our words, actions, and thoughts make up this energy. Living in loving tolerance for all living and non-living things on Earth will help us keep our heart chakras open and ascend to higher dimensional consciousness.

3. Give to others and give to the earth.

When picking up trash from the street and recycling it, we are in service to the earth. When we listen to others and give them kind words, thoughts, and actions, we are in service to humanity and, therefore, the earth because our vibrational frequency affects everything around us. Living a life in service to our environment is a good way to change our energy and dissipate any bad karma we have brought forth from a past life and to create new and better karma for ourselves in our current life and future lives.

4. **Be grateful.**

Gratitude is the fastest way to raise our vibrational frequency. Start each morning by placing one foot on the floor and saying, "Thank" and with the other foot say, "You." The words "Thank you" are great words of gratitude. We should be grateful for both good and bad experiences in our lives, for we have spiritual lessons in both.

5. **Be kind to yourself, others, and the earth.**

We are all connected. When we hurt ourselves, others, and the earth, we create a negative web of energy around our planet, which makes it harder for us to ascend to higher dimensional consciousness. Through kindness to all things in life, the negative web can be broken and ascension for all can be possible.

6. **Don't judge others; we don't know what their life's purpose is.**

We don't know what the angels have planned for another soul. As each and every person is in the various stages of progression in life, we must remember not to judge others. If we hold kindness in our hearts for all, we can walk as if we are angels on Earth as we all strive towards spiritual perfection.

7. **Be happy and be at peace.**

If we are not happy, then we will be unable to share happiness and peacefulness with others. We all have a light within and should take every opportunity to shine and hold that light on all of humanity.

8. **Identify with spiritual strength.**

Don't identify with emotions—identify with spiritual strength. Adverse circumstances should not dictate our visions of ourselves. Physical and mental hardships have to do with self-definition, but it is our spirit that actually defines who we are and what greatness we are capable of. Great power and strength does not lie with great intellect or physical prowess. Great power and strength lie within the human spirit.

To learn our spiritual lessons, we must strive in our spiritual evolution to become better than we are. Our spiritual guides were once very similar to us before they progressed. We are given imperfect bodies. Rather than concentrate only on this particular body in this specific life, we should concentrate on the spiritual growth and spiritual evolution of our soul.

Our souls chose to come to Earth to experience spiritual lessons while living in a difficult environment that involves suffering but also great beauty and promise. Our world produces brave, vigorous, and insightful souls. The great lesson of Earth is to overcome both planetary and private destructive forces in life, grow strong from the effort, move on, and spiritually evolve.

There are many great lessons to be learned while we are here. Earth appeals to our souls because of the kinship we have for each other while still struggling against one another. We compete and collaborate at the same time. Humans are egocentric but vulnerable. We can make our character mean and yet have a great capacity for kindness. There is both weak and courageous behavior here, and it is always a tug-of-war within ourselves to be strong and always do the right thing in life. We can sanction ourselves to do what is right and to help others know the endless beauty we have in our lives and how it can assist us in expressing true benevolence through our passion. Having passion to do what is right in life is worthwhile for all of humanity.

We also have a great capacity for kindness. It evolves within each and every one of us, and when we experience hard times, we can all be at our best. Through pain and suffering there can be great beauty and peace. We are all striving towards this beauty and peace.

There is much fear to overcome during our lives here. We are in conflict because of the great diversity among us, and we have not yet become open and accepting of that diversity. It is important to keep love in our hearts at all times while we are here and live by the Law of One as we are all truly connected to each other and to our Earth. Accept and embrace every person and every living and non-living thing for their diversity and uniqueness and know that we are all meant to be placed here by a higher power. Again, we don't know what someone else's soul, angels, and guides have planned for them. While we learn and evolve through our spiritual lessons and our spiritual evolution, we can all make great strides in changing who we are through these lessons and move towards spiritual perfection.

Chapter 7
Living in Abundance

What you want is irrelevant; what you've chosen is at hand.

~Spock (Star Trek)

Some souls struggle with financial issues in their everyday lives. Souls in the spirit realm have an understanding of how to manifest abundance in the universe at any time. Once on Earth, however, the third dimensional energy of consciousness is lower than the spiritual realm, and then we forget how to create what we need or what we want.

Everything we do in our home is reflected in our lives and in our body. Everything within our body, heart, and spirit is seen in our home and in our life. There is a spiritual law that states: Our body is the home of our spirit, so it is sacred, a temple to house the Divine. Our house is the home of the sacred body, the temple of our soul, and so it is an extension of the spirit's sacred space.

According to this spiritual law, we can change our life by changing our home. If we want to see changes in our heart, life, and attitude, we must change our home. By changing our home, the temple of our spirit, we can change the way our spirit is able to live within us and within our own space. Changing the energy within our home will enable us to clean up and clear out our old unneeded emotions and set our

67

intentions to live in abundance. This cleared sacred space will be the perfect place for our spirit to dwell while living here on Earth.

If we walk into our house as if we are seeing it for the first time, we can see what is ugly—what may make us feel sad, upset, tired, or frustrated. Then we can see what is beautiful—what brings us joy and reminds us of love.

If we take a few moments in each room of our home, we can be aware of what objects are present in specific places and why we placed them there. If we look around, open the closets, and peek in the basement and cabinets, we can make a few mental notes and list any observations, feelings, or emotions that arise. We should note positive and negative feelings while looking around and see what feels good in our home and enlightens our hearts and spirits when seeing it or experiencing it.

Old belongings and old emotions or thoughts attached to specific objects can be like a weight that drags us down every time we see it. We should only keep things around that are uplifting and joyful. If something is a family heirloom that has negative memories or pain attached to it, consider putting it away for a while until the painful memories have had time to heal; then bring it out again. If there are still negative emotions tied to this object or objects, then either give these items away or donate them to a charitable cause.

Cleaning out clutter allows us to open a door to the universe and make room for more things to come into our lives. By cleaning out clutter, we are making a path, so to speak, for new experiences, new opportunities, and new energy to come into our lives.

We are all empowered with special gifts. One of these gifts is the Universal Law of Creation, which states: "What we dwell upon, we create." When we have pressing issues in our lives, we put our energy into eliminating these issues that seem to come back over and over again. These scenarios might include people, situations, or complex problems that just won't go away. If we stop fighting them, thinking about them, and worrying about them, our worries will not manifest in a negative way. Again, what we dwell upon, we create, so it's always good to dwell upon and create positive circumstances and positive interactions. This way good can manifest in our lives.

Everything around us is energy; everything in the universe is made up of tiny molecules that vibrate at a specific frequency. The Law of Attraction states that *like attracts like*. For example, when strumming a guitar string, the vibration of that specific string will sound throughout the guitar and even begin to vibrate the other strings next to it. Likewise, when striking a tuning fork and placing it next to another tuning fork, it will also begin to audibly vibrate at the same frequency.

This same law can be applied to our own life and our own energy. When we give energy and vibration to our thoughts, actions, and words, it can carry itself outwards into our aura, life, and even into the universe. By giving energy, attention, thought, sound, and vibration to that which we dwell upon, we are able to create both good and bad circumstances, depending upon whether the energy is enlightening or unenlightened.

Every day of our lives, we are picking up vibrational frequencies from people and places that surround us, as well as sending out vibrational frequencies. Being peaceful is a great example of this since peace begins from within. If we love and forgive ourselves, then love and forgiveness with others will follow because what we dwell on, we create.

If we feel peaceful within our own heart, then others around us will start to *vibrate* and match this peaceful vibrational frequency just as in the situation with the guitar string and the tuning fork. We can affect so many people by keeping love and peace in our hearts at all times. This is how one person can and does change the world for the better. It all starts with what we think, what we feel, what we say, and what we focus on and give energy to. When we think or worry about something long enough, it will manifest in our lives in some way. If we shut bad situations or bad energies out of our mind and give these situations no energy, they will not manifest.

A good exercise to try is to manifest one small thing that is unusual in our day. We can write down or think about what we want to manifest. Make it something possible but unlikely to happen, such as, "Today I will see a bright green car on the freeway," or "Today I will find a quarter on the street," or "Today I will meet someone from Asia." Be realistic—it just won't be possible to manifest a polar ice cap while living in Mexico.

We can manifest most anything we want or need, but we must consider the laws that govern our world when we are trying to manifest. For example, because of the law of free will, we cannot manifest someone else's actions. When manifesting, keep in mind that we cannot bend the will of another to match our own desire. Our creations must be for the highest good of all concerned, including ourselves.

It is also possible to manifest money. Money can often be challenging to create because our angels and guides who help us manifest, see money as energy, and the paper bills we use are only paper to them. The connection between paper money and prosperity doesn't exist on the spiritual plane and can be trickier to manifest. When trying to create money, ask for *prosperity* or say, "I ask that all of my needs, bills, food, housing, clothing, transportation, etc., be generously covered and there be more than enough to meet all of my needs." This is a good prayer for financial help because it leaves it up to the angels and guides to decide how to help while still producing what we want or what we need for our highest good. Often we try to manifest money out of fear, and our angels may give us lessons about not being fearful. This may include losing all our money, so be careful when manifesting prosperity.

Monetary manifestations may come in the form of money, or they may come in the form of winning a contest for a free tune-up just when our car starts to sound funny. It could also be a new friend wanting to partner up on a gym membership. Prosperity comes in many facets, not just in monetary form.

Living in abundance isn't only about good energy flow and manifesting; it is also about staying in a positive frame of mind. How many times have we set ourselves up for failure by saying, "When X happens, then I will be happy." Life does not work this way, and angels and guides do not work this way. When creating or manifesting with angels and guides, it is important to be happy in the current moment without needing a reason for this happiness. Being happy without needing a reason to be happy is the ultimate freedom and releases us from the domination of outside influences. We are always free from having other people control us when we are happy and able to live our life in peace, happiness, and joy without restrictions.

Being happy without having a reason to be happy goes against everything our society ingrains in us. We see magazine articles telling us how to find a man or woman or how to control our man or woman into doing just what we want. Every day we view images telling us that eating this food is blissful and wearing these clothes and driving that car will bring us unending happiness. Or, having a perfect career and losing 25 pounds will make our hearts soar with glee. It is all a lie.

If we decided we were happy no matter what brand of clothes we wore, what kind of car, home, job, relationship, cereal, makeup, jewelry, vacation, or life we had, consciousness would begin to change. With a change in consciousness or our materialistic concept of happiness, businesses and corporations that feed on our fear and dissatisfaction with our lives would lose millions of dollars. Our energy is not defined by a pair of $900 shoes or an $80,000 car. Unhappiness means big money for businesses who try to convince people that a product will make them happy, rich, successful, beautiful, etc. Advertising, manufacturing, and retail businesses are forever trying to sell happiness.

Walking away from unhappiness in our lives will allow us to take back our control. Gaining greater clarity about what is truly important and getting control over our emotions will help us open our manifestation abilities to live in abundance.

It is important to clear negative energy or energy of a lower vibrational frequency from life when we are manifesting abundance. Some people can often feel drained by negative energy. Our angels and guides will assist us when we are working with souls who have a lower vibrational frequency. Energy can become drained after associating with negative people, and it can become difficult to keep our vibrational frequencies raised while being surrounded with people who have a lower vibrational frequency. This can be in our workplace, our friends, or even in our own homes.

We have great compassion within our hearts and this allows various energies to affect us. The most effective and clearest way of dealing with individuals with negative energy is to completely detach from them. If unable to completely detach, then at least emotionally detach from them by walking away or limiting contact with any person that we intuitively know is draining us.

If our mom, dad, or sister is negative, we don't give up Sunday dinners or family gatherings. Instead, we must try to be joyful in their presence and take note of our feelings while with them. Prayer is always a good way to release problems to the universe. Try a prayer such as, "Dearest Creator, I release the negativity I am carrying right now and send it into the universe to be transformed into love and peace. Please help me to return this love to everyone that I am with."

When we are feeling drained from being in a negative situation, environment, or interacting with negative people, it is good to remember to take a few moments to go outside and practice a grounding meditation. Grounding meditations are a wonderful way to calm the mind, receive messages from our angels and guides, and help transform energy. Allowing our mind to find its own inner silence and truth will help us relax, unwind, and live a life full of possibilities that can be manifested or created at any and all times.

Before meditating, find a quiet comfortable spot. Make sure the lighting is soft and play soft meditation music if desired. Be sure to take deep breaths during any meditation. Inhale through the nose for four counts and exhale through the mouth for four counts.

Here is an example of a grounding meditation:

Lie quietly and comfortably and breathe in. Now picture a beautiful white light coming down through the top of your head and out through the bottom of your feet. On the out breath, breathe deeply and let out all the worry and fear of the day. Let the bottoms of your feet connect deep down into Mother Earth. This will ground you. See white light shining down over your body from above while your feet are rooted to the center of the earth. You are here. You are safe. You are loved. It is okay to let go and know that you will be loved and taken care of by your angels and guides. All is as it should be and unfolding in the divine timing of the universe.

See yourself walking down a mountainous path to a place with tall stone walls. Go inside. The energy of your angels and guides lives here. Their love and strength fill your spirit with joy. It is a mysterious place full of wonder and light. You look up to see white light shining over you, and you feel showered with your angels and guide's love.

Now picture yourself sitting down at your computer and looking at the screen. Your angels and guides have an important message for you. What do you see on the screen? What does it say? Is there something written or a story being played out? Is there sound? Try to remember what you have seen and heard and continue walking and listening to the sound of water running. Listen to the sounds of the water along the mountainous path as you walk. You are curious and eager to see what is up ahead. The path before you turns gently into curved steps leading towards a garden. Walking gingerly along the path, you see a pool of water with a trickling stream coming from the rocks above gently dropping onto its reflective surface.

You approach the water. What do you do? Do you look into it? Do you reach towards it? Drink from it? Dive into it? Make note of your actions and ask to remember them.

Look around. There is an angel or guide who wishes to greet you on the path. Who is this being? Is the angel or guide in the water or beside it? Ask for a name. Ask if there is a message.

You sit on the bank of the pool and reflect upon the feeling of this beautiful and wondrous place. What do you feel? What do you see? Ask to remember this.

Your time has come to leave. The ones who have been with you bid you farewell. You travel back up the stone stairs. You climb up into the sunshine and feel the air on your face. You now have a clear vision of what is to come. White light shines down on you and your feet are rooted to the center of the Earth.

When you are ready, bring yourself back to the sounds of your room. Feel your arms, your shoulders, your legs, and your feet. Wiggle your fingers and your toes. When you are ready, open your eyes and remember your experience. Consider taking notes or journaling your experience.

When the turbulence of distracting thoughts subsides and our minds become still through meditation, a deep happiness and contentment naturally arises from within us. This is because we are aligning our vibrational frequency with the universe and a higher cause. This feeling of contentment and well-being helps us cope with the hectic pace and difficulties of our daily lives. So much of the stress and tension we normally experience comes from our mind, and many of the problems experienced, including ill health, are caused or aggravated by stress which can manifest in our bodies. Just by doing small meditations for ten or fifteen minutes each day, stress can be significantly reduced. Calmness and a spacious feeling in the mind can be experienced through meditation, and many problems can dissolve or will just seem to fall away.

Difficult situations can also become easier to deal with. Simple daily meditations can help us feel warm and well-disposed towards other people, and our relationships with others can gradually improve. It can also help us manifest because when our minds are calm, our request is better sent out and heard in the universe.

Meditations can be prophetic, angelic, inspiring, illuminating, or just peaceful. We never know quite what to expect. Try to connect with nature while meditating. This is important because the sophisticated person living in a city with a busy lifestyle may have lost contact with Mother Earth. Her energies empower us. Until we can see, feel the unity, and be grounded with the earth, we are missing a valuable component in our spiritual abundance and in our spiritual development.

During meditation, it is possible to connect with our angels and guides. Never be frightened or fearful when connecting with angels and guides or others who have passed on to the spiritual plane who may be trying to help us. Generally, spirits are loving beings. If we loved our grandmother when she was alive and weren't afraid of her then, why would we be afraid to see her as a loving spirit? Often she will look the same, smile at us, and try to send us a loving message. This should not be frightening but reassuring. These occurrences often spontaneously happen during meditation when they are least expected and when we are in our most relaxed state.

When we are consciously trying to contact someone in the spiritual realm, it is important that we learn specific techniques—particularly of personal protection—from books, the web, or experienced mediums or psychics. Just as there is polarity or opposites in life: dark and light, good and bad, male and female, etc., there are also negative energies in the other dimension that can frighten us or even cause us harm. Before meditating, call in an angel, such as the Archangel Michael, for guidance and protection. His blue light and spiritual sword will chase any negative entities away and protect us.

Time is speeding up as we are moving into higher dimensional consciousness. This means we are able to manifest or create very quickly. Here is a prime example of how quickly manifestations may play out:

You may decide to try manifesting a vacation to Australia. You think about it a lot and imagine yourself there, enjoying the beach and wildlife. You may not have enough money or free time to go on a vacation; however, a strange set of incidents can occur. Your boss tells you to take your vacation early because he will need you to work on an important project later in the year. A coworker tells you that she is originally from Australia and she will be visiting with family this year. She invites you to come and stay with her. Then you walk past a travel agency on the way to lunch and see a special price on airfares to Australian for the next few months.

Manifesting inexpensive accommodation, free time, and cheap airfare, and is all done subconsciously. It is also quite simple to consciously manifest what is wanted or needed in life; we just need to believe in all our possibilities.

Here are some manifesting techniques:

1. Think of the object you want and ask that it come to you "for your highest good." Be prepared to have a manifestation not work if it will do you harm instead of good, interfere with another person's free will, is not in the best interest of humanity, or is not for your highest good.

2. Put an emotional feeling behind the image of what you want. Emotion helps process manifestations more quickly. An example of these emotions could be satisfaction, joy, happiness, contentment, and love.

3. Put a visual reminder—an ad, picture, or drawing—of what you want in a prominent place, such as your bedside table.

4. Imagine that you already have the object. Feel as if it is already part of your life.

5. Have faith that it is coming to you and release it to your angels and the universe.

6. Detach from details that are absolute. For instance, if you want to manifest a red Toyota, don't refuse the offer of a green Toyota. You can always paint it red.

7. Be patient. The universe will bring the object to you in Divine timing, but it may not be by your deadline.

8. Be prepared to put some effort into attaining the object. Save half the money, enter competitions, or ask and negotiate for it.

9. Thank your angels and guides for their help and guidance.

Abundance is all around us, and our angels and guides are eagerly and tirelessly waiting to help us with everything that is for our highest good. All we have to do is ask and remember to be grateful. Being grateful is the fastest way to raise our vibrational frequency, and raising our vibrational frequency aligns us with our higher good. When we are aligned with our highest good, we are living in abundance.

Chapter 8
An Evolving Spirit

Come, let us stroll at the origin of all things.

~*Lao-tzu*

*T*here is an essential process in the universe which unfolds in our everyday lives that is difficult to understand. What does it mean to have misery on this planet? What does it mean to have death and so much pain and destruction? The answer to these questions can be found on our path or on our way through life when we walk with awareness, consciousness, and ascension.

Finding our way in life, a road, a path, the way by which we travel, is a path to our truth and our ultimate reality. Nature can never be completely understood, and this concept holds true for our own lives—for our own ultimate reality. We cannot possibly begin to think that we are in control of our lives because we have all chosen a path to walk while still in spirit.

At every moment in our lives we have a choice that will either lead us closer to our spirit or take us further away from it as we live our day-to-day lives. If we can all agree that we pick our lives before we are born and we are all ascending into higher dimensional consciousness, then we can see that ascending is evolving. We have been in a spiritual evolution just as much as a biological evolution throughout the span of space and time in each and every life that we live.

In spirit, evolving or ascending is a change in the inherited traits of our spirit from one generation to the next. These changes in our lives are caused by a combination of three processes: awareness, consciousness, and ascension. It can be said that our spiritual lessons are passed on with each generation as we reincarnate in soul groups with similar spiritual lessons to be learned here on Earth. This is the basis of our evolving spirit and the basis of our spiritual evolution.

Awareness is a term referring to our ability to perceive, to feel, or to be conscious of events, objects, or patterns. Spiritual awareness or spiritual awakening is the process by which we begin to explore our own being and our own spirit in order to become whole and reunite with our true spiritual meaning.

People seeking their spiritual paths are curious about themselves and all things around them. People of expanded spiritual awareness become engaged in the welfare of humanity and the environment. As we become more spiritually aware, we realize that we live by the Law of One—that we are all connected and if we hurt someone or something, we are only hurting ourselves. Awareness of who and what we are in our path through life opens the way for our spiritual evolution and our expansion past current, outdated beliefs.

The greatest gift of living a life in awareness is knowing that our spirit never dies. We have the inherent ability to experience all that life has to offer in all of its possibilities. It is not the destination in life but the journey or our path that makes us who we are and makes our spirit evolve. The trip itself is not about knowing but about experiencing our spiritual growth and spiritual lessons in our day-to-day lives.

These lessons and experiences are our only purpose while we're here, and it is what life is and what makes our way through life meaningful. It is our physical life that is essential in moving from our present place to a better place, and this is done through awareness. This enlightenment comes from knowing that what we dwell on, we create. In fact, we are creating and manifesting every circumstance in our lives. In this enlightenment we can come to realize that we are not pawns or victims in our awareness; we are the creators and the created. In this knowledge or awareness, we can find comfort in knowing that the joy in our lives, the joy of living, is nothing more than a buffet of experiences that we can choose from. As we become more spiritually aware with our evolving spirit, circumstances in our lives can begin to change. The beauty of our spiritual evolution and spiritual experiences is that it is a doorway for unlimited new opportunities and new experiences.

Physics tells us that everything is composed of energy. Even if we cannot see it, energy exists at various frequencies, and is, in essence, all things. Our bodies are essential in maintaining the harmony between our physical body and our spiritual body. Awareness has ramifications for us in both our physical world of mind and body and our spiritual world of our evolving soul. With this awareness we can see that there is a connection between our physical body and the soul itself. Beyond this, awareness helps us in our spiritual evolution.

Living our lives and our paths in awareness will allow us to be treated as the unique souls that we are. We are all becoming more aware whether we realize it or not. Awareness will make it possible for all of life to blossom and for all of us to manifest our dreams, live our life's purpose, and experience the life we intended to live as peaceful souls on a quest for spiritual perfection. By being aware, we move into higher dimensional consciousness and forward into our spiritual evolution. In time, through awareness, unity will allow all life to stand with compassion, love, respect, and a value of wholeness and oneness.

Consciousness is another process in which we are participating in a spiritual evolution with our evolving spirit. As time marches on, humanity is becoming more spiritual as we seek divinity and knowledge of our truth and inner worlds. As we walk our life's path, we are also attaining enlightenment.

Some feel that a higher power exists and that we are all connected to something bigger than just ourselves. One day we may come to realize that we all worship the same or a similar Divine presence in different forms and approaches, and we are all of the same essence. As we walk our path, we can only hope that eventually there will be a time when we will feel an awakening among humanity, so we can live among our similarities and differences without fear, hatred, and war.

Consciousness can be a difficult term to define because it is used and understood in a variety of ways. What one person sees as a definition of consciousness can be seen by others as something completely different. Consciousness may involve thoughts, sensations, perceptions, moods, emotions, dreams, and self-awareness.

In order to be in a place of higher dimensional consciousness, we must become fully conscious. This means stopping old patterns and habits that prevent us from living in heightened awareness. There are many means for bringing our soul into the light of higher consciousness. Our angels work tirelessly behind the scenes to help us strive for or bask in the light of this consciousness.

The angels say that if 55% of the population is conscious about something, it can be changed. When working consciously on issues, it doesn't mean we are just thinking about it; it means we are doing something about it. That is, we can either think about recycling our trash, or we can be conscious of this issue and actually do it. The actual act of recycling makes us conscious about it.

As our souls have been shifting towards enlightenment through our spiritual evolution, we are already beginning to see great changes that are happening for the better. Many of us are living our lives in consciousness because we want to make changes for the better in our lives on Earth.

One of the most common experiences of spiritual consciousness is the feeling of *oneness*. Oneness is often experienced as a feeling that everything is part of a whole or that we all come from one common source, share a common spirit, and are all connected. Our spiritual experiences in life are expressed by our perceptions. We should accept good things that happen in life as well as the bad things because there are spiritual lessons in both scenarios. Through the conscious feeling of oneness, we are able to rise to a higher level of consciousness and come to understand that the difference between good and bad is not what we normally perceive. They are both beneficial to us in some way.

Through awareness and consciousness, we are able to understand that seemingly bad things that happen to us serve an important purpose. The purpose is to help us and the world around us with our spiritual evolution. If we look at all the challenging situations in our lives, we can understand that at the end of our life's work, both good and bad experiences are all for our highest good.

Looking back over the course of our lives we can see that difficult experiences we have gone through were often a doorway to a new beginning or opportunity. If we can carry into our daily lives a consciousness that goes beyond the concept of good and bad, we can then operate from a centered platform. This will enable us to make better decisions for ourselves because we can see the world with a greater depth and a deeper truth.

Spiritual consciousness can be maintained on a daily basis by beginning each day with our thoughts, words, and actions being in a place of peace. This positive daily practice will keep us aware of spiritual principles that we should be incorporating into our lives, such as the Law of One and the Golden Rule. Our relationship to our own spiritual consciousness is a direct relationship to the development of our spiritual evolution. Spiritual evolution is why we are here and why we have been coming back here over and over again.

Ascension is the third process in our path in life to our spiritual evolution. If ascension is evolving, then ascension is indeed evolution. We are all ascending into higher dimensional consciousness as a civilization and are in the midst of an incredibly powerful spiritual evolution whether we realize it or not.

Our Earth is ascending to higher dimensional consciousness and we as her children must ascend with her, or she will make us change. Mother Nature will execute her plan one way or another in this ascension or shift.

Through awareness, we can align ourselves with a higher source and keep vibrational frequencies at a higher level to help us live our life's purpose and find the special gifts and talents we have to offer this world.

There is a famous parable that goes something like this:

A man walked along the seashore and saw a boy picking something up from the sand and throwing it into the sea. The man came closer and saw that the boy was picking up starfish; he was completely surrounded by them. It seemed like there were millions of starfish on the sand, for the shore was literally filled with them for many miles ahead.

"Why are you throwing these starfish in the water?" asked the man, as he approached the boy.

"If they stay on the shore until the morning tide, they will die," answered the boy without interrupting what he was doing.

"But this is stupid!" yelled the man. "Look around you! There are millions of starfish here; the shore is filled with them. Your efforts won't make any difference!"

The boy picked up the next starfish, thought for a moment, then threw it into the sea, and said, "No, my efforts will change a lot for *this* starfish."

Then the man also picked up a starfish and threw it into the sea. And then another one. By the time the night was over, there were many people on the shore, and each of them were picking up and throwing starfish into the sea. When the sun rose, the shore was empty, and no starfish was left unsaved.

Since our actions have a great influence on the world, we should engrave in our memory the words of Joan Walsh Anglund: "One seed can start a garden; one drop can start a sea; one doubt can start a hating; one dream can set us free."

Our soul and our spirit care about the joy of being and experiencing what is in front of us. Thoughts create our experiences and our emotional state manifests into being through these thoughts. Whatever we put out mentally, we will get back energetically because our physical reality is a reflection of our mental reality.

It is better for our soul to have a bad experience to learn and grow from than no experience at all. Those that try to run from experiencing things, doing things, and creating things will be unable to spiritually grow and evolve in their paths as an evolving spirit. Whatever it is we give off energetically, we can get back in any form. How we define ourselves energetically is reflected back to us from our own reality so we can decide whether we wish to retain a specific idea and frequency or to change it. The conscious choice is always ours to make. We must be careful because, often energetically, we don't see things as they truly are; we see things as we are.

We should not be surprised when our lives change after requesting or manifesting something we want or need. Angels are amazed that we ask for change and when our life starts changing, we become uncomfortable because we lose our job, our friends, and all the old baggage that we have been carrying around—and then turn to fear. We often fail to understand that as our changes begin, there is an evolution of consciousness that is cleaning house and getting rid of old energy to make way for new and better energy.

We can help manifest anything we want or need in our path in life by placing an order with the universe. We can climb a flight of stairs to the top of the building and throw our wish or request out to the universe. There is then a new vibrational frequency being sent out. If we start to worry about our request and think about how it hasn't happened yet, we don't deserve it, or we're not good enough for it, we then drop out of the vibrational frequency. Then our request comes back to the roof top, but because of our doubts, we have dropped down to a lower floor or lower vibrational frequency. We dropped out of the frequency in which our request exists. It is important to stay at the same vibrational frequency in which we placed our order and believe that it will come to fruition. We must also accept the changes that come to our lives with our requests without fear.

Finding our way as an evolving spirit is not easy. We are searching for direction, our purpose in life, and our spiritual path. Our soul's journey is long and is rarely easy. Everything worthwhile in our lives requires hard work and, many times, pain and frustration. An important prerequisite to finding our path and our way is in the willingness to be open and honest with ourselves and staying true to our spirits. By being willing to release that which we find is no longer good on our path, we can understand the shifts that can create a sense of disruption and upheaval necessary to our spiritual growth. We choose how we will walk our path in this life. Fear creates stagnation; openness creates expansion. It is up to us to exercise our free will along with the forces of destiny to manifest our dreams and our true spiritual purpose.

There are many lessons to be learned if we are to continually learn and grow in our spiritual evolution. We should be thankful for whatever is in our life, both good and bad, for it is there as a teacher. Some situations feel like punishment and make us question why they are happening to us. What did we do to deserve this in our life? It's not so much about deserving it but rather recognizing the patterns that are continually repeated and then making a conscious decision to change them.

Different aspects and experiences in our lives can converge to create an overall picture of who we are and what our place is in this world. Conflict is inevitable, both internally and externally. It is our reactions to these struggles that define us as a person. By understanding our spirits, we can increase our trust in the decisions we make and the paths we choose to follow. Each of us must find our own way in our lives.

The Chinese philosopher Lao Tzu writes about a path in life, a way to higher consciousness. It is called, "The Way."

The Way that can be experienced is not true;
The world that can be constructed is not true.
The Way manifests all that happens and may happen;
The world represents all that exists and may exist.
To experience without intention is to sense the world;
To experience with intention is to anticipate the world.
These two experiences are indistinguishable;
Their construction differs but their effect is the same.
Beyond the gate of experience flows the Way,
Which is ever greater and more subtle than the world.

As Lao Tzu says, "I find good people good. And I find bad people good when I am good enough."

Remember, we are all affecting the world at every moment, whether we mean to or not. Our actions and states of mind matter because we are so deeply interconnected with one another. Working on our own consciousness and our own path in life is the most important thing that we can do at any moment as an evolving spirit. We can arise and awaken within our consciousness our memories of all the lives we have lived. We can arise and awaken to our true meaning and our true spiritual purpose. We can arise and awaken to the joys and wonders of this life and our spiritual evolution.

Chapter 9

Connecting To Humanity

All things are connected. Whatever befalls the Earth befalls the children of the Earth.
~Chief Seattle, Suqwamish and Duwamish

Not everyone in this world can laugh, but we can all certainly feel pain and are all connected to each other through this pain. If we think about pain being a large piece of pie, when we divide that pie up evenly among everyone in the world, then nobody has a large burden. That is, we all share a little bit of it equally. It is this pain that helps us spiritually grow and advance and is specific to our world. Souls that choose to come to Earth are brave souls indeed. When done reincarnating here on this tough playground called Earth, we will be well-equipped to go on to do great things in this and other universes.

We share an energetic field here on Earth. It links us all together, and this is why when we have a shift in consciousness, it moves through us all and changes the way we feel and see our lives. We were made to be strong with each other and interlink to divinity through the intertwining of our hearts and souls. When alone, we can find each other. Through each other, we can find ourselves and this helps connect us.

At times, the most painful lives can be the most creative and the most productive ones. Pain makes us more insightful and brings us closer to our spiritual lessons and closer to each other. Through our pain, we can connect to each other by respecting life. We share our common humanity by being tolerant and generous amongst ourselves and each other.

Change is possible within each of us. We can overcome conflict and hatred, spanning seemingly timeless generations, and live in peace. We can grow and rise above limitations in stagnant and outdated non-spiritual beliefs and policies that hurt our world as a whole.

There are times when we feel that even if we are surrounded by other people in our lives, we are alone. We might feel that we're going through this difficult journey called life by ourselves, no matter if we're married, have children, or close family and friends. In the end, it is important to remember that we are never alone. Our angels and guides are always with us, helping and guiding us with our Divine lessons on this tough playground called Earth.

By knowing that our angels and guides are with us and by connecting with other human beings, we can overcome feelings of loneliness. When we connect with each other, we are no longer alone. We share our suffering, our experiences, and our common trials. The obstacles we face in life are no longer insurmountable when we have someone to face them with whether it's a family member, a friend, or a chat group on the web.

By being tolerant, loving unconditionally, and caring for others, we can give joy and direction in our lives. If we see others as spiritual beings acting out a play in physical bodies, we can become more aware of our *part* in our life and the lives of others while we all advance in our lessons. Being kind and gentle towards others is a good way to lead our lives towards spiritual advancement and reap the effects of good karma. Living life with happiness and forgiveness will help us discover our heart and soul's purpose and will also help us connect to each other. If we live our beliefs and philosophy and trust the universe, we will discover we are all loved and guided in the best possible way through Divine presence. Through this, we can move towards our greatest potential, sharing whatever our unique gifts we have to offer humanity.

One practical way of living as a spiritual being is through awareness. By being aware of every situation that arises in life and not reacting emotionally towards controversial situations we encounter, we can better understand the value of our spiritual lessons. When an argument arises, we can step back and look at everyone concerned and ask, "How would an angel or guide react?" An angel or guide would react with gentleness, forgiveness, and love. Not with anger, hate, or spite. We must see the higher view and ask, "Is this argument really important? Is there another way to deal with this issue?" When we lash out in anger, our spiritual lessons and advancement are lost. Often these situations arise over and over because there is a lesson to be learned.

We must learn to release problems and difficult situations to the universe. By doing this, we leave it up to our angels and guides to decide how to solve our problems in a way that will be for our highest good. Each time we do this, the problems will become easier to relinquish. Soon this process will become automatic, which will make it easier to release ourselves from challenging people and situations.

Everything in our lives happens for a reason and is in accordance with Divine timing. There are spiritual lessons to be learned from each and every situation we encounter, whether the experience is good or bad. All people should be treated with equal respect, as we are all here on Earth for the same reason, our spiritual evolution.

For all of us living our lives in higher dimensional consciousness, incarnating on Earth at this time is a great adventure. Many lightworkers are here on a group project, arriving as teachers and healers for our planet. Lightworkers are here to wake us up and to help us recognize our life's purpose and will do whatever is necessary to shock us into conscious awareness. They are also here to remind us to have fun—something we forget to incorporate in our lives from time to time.

We need to affirm and help each other with our *mission* and our spiritual evolution, and we can do this by connecting to each other. The purpose of conscious evolution for the human race as a whole is to create a "New Earth." With the assistance from our angels, guides, and each other, we can rediscover our oneness, our common humanity.

This knowledge can be used to raise our consciousness and begin to create a new Earth. This will be a place where all living beings can thrive and be respected for who they are—one where we will respect each other's similarities and differences and live in loving tolerance of those similarities and differences. We should always celebrate the incredible diversity that characterizes our oneness and makes life an adventure in consciousness. Peace must also be made within ourselves in order to make peace in the world and to connect with humanity.

Teachers of conscious awareness have been arriving to assist us with our ascension for a long time. They are spiritual warriors whose function is to clear the old systems so that new ideas and ways of doing things can be created. They are the systems busters who will liberate us from our old ways of thinking and aid in connecting us to each other.

These teachers do this by incarnating into our families and communities. They bring with them their gifts of advanced spiritual development, a high level of consciousness, and wisdom. They are spiritually aware and awake and refuse to allow themselves to be constrained or enslaved by impersonal beliefs.

They show us that gentle, wise and high-level beings cannot flourish and thrive in the systems we have created and that we need to work together, as one, to bring about change. The high level of dysfunction in our society is a signal that we need to change to accommodate ourselves as spiritual beings of higher vibrational frequency and multi-dimensional consciousness.

Karma is also important when connecting to humanity. Every thought we have, every word that we speak either adds to or takes away from the light of humanity. Everything we think and say about ourselves, whether it is silently to ourselves or aloud to others, either adds to or takes away from the light of humanity. Everything we think and say to and about others, whether it is silently to ourselves or aloud to others, either adds to or takes away from the light of humanity. There are no insignificant thoughts or words; each one has energy and an effect.

When our thoughts and words come from a space of unconditional love and non-judgment, they spread light and increase the light and vibrational frequency on the planet. When they come from fear or anger, they take away from the light. Our thoughts and words make a difference, and each one is important. Even the smallest judgment or thought has an effect. Each person is as important as another in spreading the light and connecting to others.

Just as we are discovering our power to create miracles and manifest our reality, we must also realize that this power extends to all parts of our being, including and especially our thoughts and words. This affects everyone around us. We do not have insignificant thoughts, so we should carefully guard our thoughts and words. We must release anger, fear, and judgment from our lives. These feelings block our energy and keep us at a lower vibrational frequency on the old energy grid which prevents us from ascending.

Learning to let go of old, ineffective energy patterns and adapting to change is also important when connecting to humanity. Reaction to change is often tinged with suspicion, caution, or resistance, and adapting to change involves give and take. We have to let go of something to gain something. Holding onto old energy can block our auras and slow our progression with spiritual advancement. Great beauty and opportunity are within us when we connect to humanity.

Forgiveness is the foundation of all spiritual work and growth because it is through awareness that we can truly know our own life's journey and perspective. Forgiveness is not a process of giving something to another person, who may not deserve anything, but it is instead a process of turning our energy inward and using the power of love to look closely at our relationships with others and ourselves. When anchored in forgiveness, we are all within the spiritual realm of conscious awareness rather than in the realm of emotions or the mind.

It is natural to release old energy because holding onto it hinders the flow of love into our own life and blocks our spiritual balance and peace. Love is the energy that gives and maintains life. Forgiving others, even those who don't seem to deserve it, can bring life-giving energy into our bodies.

We all have bad energy in our auras and in our hearts that create challenges and blockages in our lives that prevent us from connecting to each other. We are all in the process of learning how to clear these issues, entities, thought forms, fears, and old wounds from our bodies and our hearts so that we can all ascend and become the enlightened beings that we are meant to be—connected to each other throughout humanity. Conscious awareness and connecting to humanity can also be obtained through faith. Great teachers of the world, such as Buddha, derived their strength and inspiration not from muscle or intellect but from faith. Buddha spoke a great language that went straight to people's hearts. We are no different. Great spiritual teachers of the world speak and connect to us through our heart chakras and ask us to have faith.

This is a critical time in humanity's spiritual evolution, and we are all connected on a spiritual level. We are all here to build and spread the light for all of humanity. We can be a light and spread our own light by focusing our intention on what we want in life. When we focus on what others have, we are seeing our life from a point of lack. By focusing our energy on what we want, we bring the light into our life and then spread the light to others. Each of us is important to the task that we have come to do. The result of our energy is continuously manifested all around us. If we take this power that has been taught to us and use it wisely, we can spread our light throughout the world. If we use it well, we can create heaven on Earth for ourselves and for all of humanity through conscious awareness.

Mahatma Gandhi once said that an "eye for an eye" would leave everybody blind. It is no secret that our planet has reached a global crisis as we are living among systems that no longer serve the good of humanity. If we take a close look at the world around us, we can see that the world is becoming more impoverished. The rich are getting richer, and the poor are getting poorer and taken advantage of. It is wonderful to have the things we need in life, but we must never forget that we all share a common home, our planet and a common race, humanity.

When we continue to fill our landfills and fail to recycle, we trash our planet in the name of development. As a group we can shift our consciousness and our world to a place where peace and love will change the planet. It is more important now than ever to help nurture ourselves and each other. Without group consciousness, we are all going to hell in a hand basket, so to speak.

Our planet has reached a crisis of epoch proportions. We, as her children, have reached a point of stagnation in our growth. We have hemmed ourselves in with systems that have become impersonal and no longer function for the greater good of humanity. More and more of the world's people are becoming impoverished in both material and spiritual terms as a small minority accumulates more power and wealth for itself. We continue to trash our planet in the name of development and to kill each other in senseless wars often fought in the name of religion and freedom.

We are in a state of crisis. The systems that have been set up by us to create a stable society have become stagnant and repressive. Systems such as economics, health, law, and education are no longer serving communities and the people that they were originally designed to serve. These systems have become self-serving and are now destructive and harmful. These systems are fueled by greed and money.

Humanity, in general, has lost the spiritual dimension of life and is focused on the lower chakra areas of money, sex, and power. Consumption has become a goal in life in the developed world. Those beliefs and concepts are spreading around the planet, producing a society based on greed and materialism and not one of unity and oneness.

This is the state of our world today. By shifting our consciousness and connecting to humanity, we can be more conscious of what we are doing to ourselves and how we need to change our community life in order to create more nourishing, peaceful, and loving situations that will foster our continued growth as humans.

We have come to this planet to grow and learn our spiritual lessons. But we have also come with a specific purpose—to help the planet with its spiritual evolution by raising our energy and consciousness and by connecting to each other.

Messages we are receiving at this time from the universe are messages of the heart. As a group we are working to help humanity open its collective heart chakra and embrace higher energy and higher consciousness. We are also creating a new society based on love and empowerment. It is a society that exists beyond duality in the realm of oneness.

Through our lives, we are learning the skills of intention, focus, and manifestation, and we are also learning that the true meaning of happiness is not individual greed but a collective need for sharing and an appreciation of oneness.

If there is one thing we have always had and will always have, it is hope. Hope is the most incredible word. This word not only means to wish for something but to wait with expectation for its fulfillment. It is an emotional belief in a positive outcome related to events and circumstances within one's personal life. It is a belief that there will be a positive outcome even when there is evidence to the contrary.

As aware and conscious spiritual beings, it is important to hold the light not only on ourselves but also on those who will not or don't know how to change their energy. We all made an agreement before we were born as to what our purpose is and how we were going to live our lives to achieve that purpose and help humanity. We don't know what these agreements are for others or what role they chose to play in the Divine plan of things. So we must be careful not to judge others and to be kind to all, even people who are not kind to us, and we will be truly be happy. If we stay connected to humanity through our spiritual evolution, anything can be possible in our lives and on Earth.

Chapter 10
Path of Awakening

You can't wake a person who is pretending to be asleep.

~ Native Proverb

*T*here is a path of awakening which leads to the heart of the universe. On this path we learn who we are, what we are doing here, and where we are going. Others may point the way, but it is we who actually obtain knowledge and develop the wisdom needed to awaken our inner consciousness and awareness.

Discovering and understanding our path helps us to comprehend pieces of knowledge and their impact on our lives and the lives of others. During our journey, we can see the implications of our decisions and how specific actions may affect others and the world around us.

Deep within our spirits the knowledge obtained in our consciousness is transformed into awareness and feelings of peaceful coexistence. Through our wisdom, we are able to apply principles that allow us to work in harmony with each other.

Through careful observation and vigilant attention to our thoughts and actions, we will become more meaningful and considerate creators of our own lives and more unselfish forces in others' lives. It is our path, and we each are literally the path we seek.

The path we lead, the path of awakening to all things in life, begins with a few simple steps and the understanding that we all have a purpose. We need to live our lives in consciousness and in awareness of our karma as we have many spiritual lessons to be learned in conjunction with karmic lessons. Jason Johns runs the Phoenix Transformational Therapy practice in the UK. Jason talks about important life principles of ancient wisdom and spiritual practices to provide individuals a holistic approach to their personal growth. Jason talks about basic principals in life that can bring our body, mind, and spirits on a path that will awaken our spirit within. This is important when walking to or being on the path of awakening that we are all mindful and conscious of our lives and all living things around us.

The following are some principles to help guide us down our path of awakening:

1. **Everything in life is related**. Native American writings and most religions that are based on earth-centered philosophies say we are all related in life. If we treat ourselves with love, respect, and compassion, we will have that same love, respect, and compassion for all things on Earth and in life. We are all part of the same whole; we are all rowing the same boat, so to speak. Our souls have the capability to find a way to allow our spirits to shine with great light and intensity by just being who we are and understanding that we are here for a reason.

2. **The universe is composed of energy**. The energy of the universe flows among, between, and within everything around us. When we have internal blocks, our energy fails to flow correctly within our meridians. This causes illness, disease, and other

99

symptoms in our bodies. When our meridians flow freely, our energy promotes health, prevents disease, and cures illness. This energy, or chi, can be directed consciously in a manner in which we can see it and feel it. Our thoughts, words, and actions make up our aura or energy field and what we think, say, and do affect this aura or energy field. For example, negative actions and thoughts can drain energy while positive actions and thoughts can create good energy.

3. **We are beings of both spirit and human nature**. We are spiritual beings, but at the same time, we are souls living on Earth. We inhabit both worlds simultaneously even though we are often unaware of it. We should embrace both our physical and spiritual realm as both are equally important. We have to walk with one foot in each of these worlds with the understanding that they go hand-in-hand with the cycles of reincarnation and karma. Neglecting either our spiritual or earthly side can cause distress and misunderstanding of our true purpose. Remembering that we have agreed to come here from the spiritual realm can help us stay focused on mastering our spiritual lessons.

4. **No one soul is superior to another**. No one being or creature is any better or of more importance than another—we are all the same. We are all in various stages of our spiritual evolution and have different levels of understanding. This does not make any one person better than another, and we should never judge others as we are unaware of their lessons. We are not masters of nature, plants, or animals. They are our companions and co-inhabitants of our planet. We are not superior to any other living thing nor do we own them. We are simply the caregivers of this planet

and should treat everyone and everything with love, understanding, compassion, and respect.

5. **Belief creates**. What we dwell on, we create. How we perceive the universe is shaped by our beliefs, and if we believe we are in a hurry, then everyone else appears to be moving slowly. Through belief and positive thought, we can create or manifest anything we want or need for our higher good or the higher good of others. We should always believe in our abilities and ourselves. If we believe in our spirit, we will succeed. If we can combine the power of belief with that of manifestation, we can bring anything into our reality.

6. **Trust our intuition**. Inside of us, a voice speaks and guides us. This is our intuition, and it is often guided by our higher self, angels, and guides. We can choose to ignore our intuition or we can choose to listen to it. Once we are in tune with our intuition and start listening to it, we will be guided and will find that any goal is achievable in our lives. When we realize that Spirit works through us, it will be to our benefit. Our angels, guides, and higher self will always help guide us in our lives when asked and are always working for our highest good.

7. **There is a higher purpose**. Everything that happens in our lives happens for a reason and for our greater good. We have to learn to look at events in our lives from more than just a normal human perspective. We must see these events from an elevated spiritual platform and look at what spiritual lessons and spiritual growth will come from both good and bad events in our lives. All is as it should be in life. There is no such thing as accidents. Everything is in compliance with Divine timing.

8. **There are no ordinary moments**. The past only exists as our memory, and the future only exists as our expectation. The only moment in time that counts is now, this moment. Every moment in life is precious, and we should treat it as such and live each moment to the fullest because by being in the present, we have presence. To live in the now, the conscious mind should be quiet and focused on what we are doing, not what we are doing next week or what happened yesterday. The past is no longer there; the future is not here yet. There is only one moment in which life is meant to be lived, and that is the present moment.

9. **There are no limits**. The only limits we have are those we place upon ourselves or others place upon us, and to this end, we should avoid being limited by others. If someone views a dog as being aggressive, then it is more likely to be aggressive. Holding expectations of others and limiting them, stunts spiritual growth. What we think about we manifest, and what we visualize we create. If we make our manifestations and creations positive and enlightening, then life will be without limitations and our souls can soar.

10. **Action not reaction is important**. If we are tickled, our reaction is to laugh. Living in a state of awareness where we do not react in any given situation, but act instead reflects a life living in consciousness. Reaction is unconscious whereas action is conscious, and we should not let past influences affect our current actions. There are times to act, as well as times to be still. By living in the present moment and having control of our conscious mind, we can better direct our actions and, therefore, our lives.

11. **Positivity rules**. Negative thoughts attract negative actions, situations, and people and can create bad karma. Positive thoughts attract positive actions, situations, and people and can create good karma. We should look at our thoughts and the events that happen to us in a positive light, recognize negative thoughts for what they are, and release them to the universe. By remaining positive and seeing the good in all people and all situations, we can create a reality where a light will always shine upon us.

12. **Posture, pose, and breathing help maintain life**. Energy flows through our bodies as it flows through all things in life. If our posture and pose are incorrect, our energy cannot flow clearly; this creates blockages that can manifest as pain or illness. We breathe in energy from the world around us; therefore, our breaths should be deep and full, coming from the bottom of the belly and not the chest. This enables us to maximize our energy and helps us to relax. When we are stressed, angry, or afraid, our breathing changes and becomes shallow and fast. By consciously controlling our breathing and keeping it deep and even, we can release stress, anger, or fear, so we can act consciously from an elevated platform in whatever situation we are in.

13. **Keep everything in balance**. The universe exists in a state of balance, as should we. We can do almost anything we wish, but should always do it in moderation—never in excess and always in consciousness of all living and non-living things in this world. Anything in excess can become addictive, which drains energy. Staying balanced in our lives allows us to keep and maintain a higher vibrational frequency.

14. **Intent is action**. We can intend to do anything, and our intent is important. However, unless the intent is followed with action, the intent will not come to fruition. For example, we may intend to get fit but spend our time watching TV, eating pizza, and drinking Coke. We have intention, but our actions do not confirm or create the intention; therefore, we must use actions to create or manifest what we want. If action turns knowledge into wisdom, then consciousness is intent with action. We can be mindful of something, but unless we put action into that thought, it is not conscious and consciousness helps raise our vibrational frequency.

15. **Freedom of choice is free will**. We all have free will and can choose to do almost anything we wish. There is no situation in life where we do not have a choice. Sometimes it takes a great amount of courage and strength to make the right decisions in life. We have the courage of conviction and power of spirit to make any decisions necessary to lead us on a good karmic path when we are mindful of our spiritual lessons. There is a good karmic piggy bank and a bad karmic piggy bank. At the end of our lives it is important that our thoughts, words, and actions have a positive and conscious influence on all that we do.

16. **Change happens**. Change is continuous and is always happening around us. We cannot always perceive change, but we can see the end result of it. Change is not a bad thing, nor should it be feared. Through change we can grow and move forward in our lives, learning our spiritual lessons along the way. If we chose not to change, we will become stagnant in our spiritual growth and, therefore, our spiritual evolution.

17. **Take responsibility for our actions**. Actions can cause reactions. It is the Law of Cause and Effect. For every action there is an equal and opposite reaction, including a karmic boomerang. We have to be aware of our actions, take responsibility for them, and be conscious of their consequences. When being critical, judgmental, or unsupportive of others, we are lowering our vibrational frequency and creating bad karma. By taking responsibility for our own actions, we can take back the power of our spirit and the freedom to choose good thoughts, words, and actions, which in turn creates good karma.

18. **One step at a time**. To achieve any goal in life, it should be broken down into a number of smaller steps. If we have many small successes, this can lead to larger successes. If we aim for large goals too quickly, we may fail. Remember that every journey begins with a single step, then a second, and a third and as many steps required until we reach our destination. We should reward and praise ourselves for all our successes, however big or small they are. What we dwell on we create, so manifest many goals in life and achieve success one step at a time.

19. **Never sit in judgment**. We have no right to judge others for their words, thoughts, or actions because we don't know what their spiritual lessons are. We have the freedom of choice to do as we please and act as we wish, and it is up to us to live our lives either consciously or unconsciously. We are in no position to judge anyone, as we are imperfect souls striving in our spiritual evolution, and by judging others, we lower our vibrational frequency. Everyone has a life's purpose and we don't know what that life purpose is or what spiritual lessons that we, our guides, or our angels have pre-planned for ourselves or others.

20. **It is all about integrity**. Integrity is how we act when no one else is looking—it is the concept of consistency of actions, values, and principles. We must live by our own standards and should not judge others by these standards. Our lives are about living in conjunction with our highest spiritual intentions. Being kind, living our lives with integrity, and always doing the right thing is spiritually rewarded and helps us with our spiritual progression.

21. **Failure is not an option**. People that succeed in life never give up and never stop trying until they reach their goal—failure is never an option. Success often does not come easy and does require hard work. Most overnight successes have been from people manifesting and working hard towards their goals and dreams for many years. Failure is not something to be feared because we can never fail. Everything we do, no matter whether we view it as a success or failure, holds a valuable spiritual lesson for us. By looking at a perceived failure as a valuable lesson, it no longer feels bad and becomes a success. The only true failure is not learning our lessons or mistakes life has taught us. By changing our thoughts and the way we perceive ourselves and the world around us as successful, we can change our lives.

22. **Life is an ongoing journey**. Our journeys and explorations through life never stop. In truth, they continue for many lifetimes. The destination is not the reward or the goal in our spiritual evolution; it is the journey to the destination that is the goal itself. The spiritual lessons learned are always our rewards, and we should not forget that our angels and guides want us

to have fun in all our journeys along our life's path.

23. **Change our mind**. If we take an objective view of our mind, then we can see that many thoughts drift through it, many of which we are unaware. A sad, angry, or fearful thought may drift up from the subconscious and change how we feel for no apparent reason. If we take control of our minds through tools such as meditation and become aware of these thoughts, we can realize them for what they are. Then we can release them to the universe, while remaining relaxed, calm, and centered. By consciously focusing our minds, we can release negative energy and change our minds from negative thought patterns to positive thought patterns.

24. **Emotions come and go**. Emotions flow through us at all times, often without us realizing it. Many of us do not express our emotions because we feel we have to act or behave in a specific manner. When we feel negative emotions, we can feel our bodies become tense; if we do not express these emotions when we feel them, the tension is stored within our bodies, energy, and aura. Having emotions should not be feared but should be celebrated. When we feel an emotion, we should express it. If we are happy, we should smile and laugh, and if we are sad we should cry. Expressing our emotions releases tension and helps us live more fully in the current moment. Once we have expressed an emotion, it is gone and will not return with the same force for that specific situation. If we refuse to express our emotions, then like damming a fast river, eventually the water level will rise too high. It must be provided with an outlet. We can always release the energy of our emotions out of our bodies and let the universe take care of them.

25. **Don't forget to play and laugh**. As children, we play exuberantly. We have fun, enjoy ourselves, and have lots of energy. Then something happens. We grow up and we no longer play, believing that adults have to act like adults and adults don't play. Playing is one of our greatest joys and sources of pleasure in life. It takes many forms, from sports to games to laughing and joking with friends. Playing increases our energy and keeps us in a positive frame of mind. It makes those around us more positive and generally lifts the spirits of all involved. There are times to be serious, yes, but there are times to play, too, and that is what we must remember.

If we live simply, love generously and care deeply, we will truly find a path to awakening.

Chapter 11
Angels Among Us

I can believe anything, provided that it is quite incredible.

~Oscar Wilde

ngelology is the study of angels. It comes from the Greek word "Angelologia," which is a combination of two words: "angelos" meaning angel or messenger and "ology," which is the science or study of—thus, the science or study of angels. In Christian, Muslim, Jewish, and other theologies, an angel is depicted as one who acts as a messenger, attendant, or agent of God. Throughout the Bible, the will of God is usually imparted or carried out by angels.

Angels are spirits without bodies who possess superior intelligence, gigantic strength, and surpassing holiness. Angels are composed of ethereal matter, thus allowing them to take on whichever form best suits their immediate needs to work with us on our spiritual lessons in our lives. They are the essence of love and joy and stem from the heart of God. They are countless in their number and flock around the universe in their millions, helping all spiritual beings that ask for their love and guidance.

Angels are dedicated to serving the needs of all spiritual beings so that we may experience the same level of unconditional love as they do. Each angel carries out its assigned task without any hint of hesitation as they take great joy and pleasure in offering their loving wisdom and guidance to all beings in all universes.

Without exception, all of us have angels around us constantly, and they are eager and excited at the opportunity to communicate with us. Most of us have one to three angels assigned to us our whole life or for many lifetimes, but additional angels will come and go as we work on our spiritual lessons. Angels were created with one purpose—to love and to serve without conditions. In doing so, angels hold a focus of pure love throughout the universe and are able to set up a resonance for the vibration of pure love wherever and whenever it is needed.

Here on Earth, we have free will. This means that we have chosen to gain our experiences through many lifetimes and many varied forms of existence. Our angels are created to counterbalance any energies or actions that move in the opposite direction to love so that we will remember our true spiritual purpose. Love is all around us every day of our lives; we only need to open our eyes to see it, feel it, and experience it.

When we think of angels, we often think of a beautiful figure with white wings wearing a long flowing robe. We also see them with halos that emanate from the angels' heads in a glorious wreath of light, serving as a symbol of divine wisdom.

Angels can appear to us in many forms and shapes. At times, the qualities of an angel are so delicate that they come in specific forms that will suit our needs. An angel will often appear to us with the form that is best for us or one that we can understand.

Angels do not die or age; they are immortal, created by God and have been in existence since the beginning of time. They are thought of as the guardians of souls and can take on a variety of different forms. In Ezekiel 1:16–21, Isaiah 6:1–3, and throughout the book of Revelation, they are described as taking on not only the appearance of men but many phenomenal forms. A notable example was the angel who took on the appearance of a burning bush. The actual image of an angel with wings tends to symbolize the spiritual nature of all beings. The wings allow the angel to travel through time and space and serve as a symbol of divine authority.

Angels are everywhere, and we can ask for angels to assist us with anything we wish that is for our higher purpose or higher good. There is no limit. There is an angel available for any particular task, and they come to us as an answer to our wishes and prayers. We are able to order an angel in order to request anything we want, need, wish, or desire. We can order a parking angel to help us park at the mall at Christmas time. We can order an angel to help us with a test at school or a troubled relationship. We can even order an accounting angel. The possibilities are endless, and they want to come into our lives and help no matter how small or irrelevant our task may seem.

It is important to remember that angels cannot just come into our lives when we need help. We must specifically ask for their help. It is also important to be grateful and say thank you for their divine wisdom, love, help, and support in our lives because being grateful for both good and bad things raises our vibrational frequency.

On a personal note, I have an ancient angel that has come to me in many instances of my life during turbulent times. She appears to me as a large liquid form of mercury in an oval shape and is approximately 4 feet long and 3 feet wide. My angel will sit a few feet over my body while I tell her my troubles. Every time she is with me, she seems to "zap" me with a sort of fuzzy crooked lightning bolt. The lightning bolt always hits me around or just below my belly button. The zap doesn't hurt, but it doesn't feel good either; it just is. This zap literally jolts my whole body up and off the bed. After I am zapped, the most incredible feeling instantly comes over me. I have the most amazing feeling of such love and peace for all things in the universe that it is almost indescribable. I believe this is the feeling that we experience when we pass over to the spiritual realm. Within a few seconds I then drift off to sleep.

If you have a loved one that has passed over, please know that they are truly at peace. The feeling that I feel inside my heart and soul after my "zap" can only be described as utter bliss. The love felt for all things in the universe extends even to rapists, murderers, etc. It doesn't matter what or who it is; there is nothing but pure, unconditional, undefined love.

Another type of angel with us during our life is our guardian angel. A guardian angel is an angelic being that is dedicated to serve and to help us throughout our lifetime. However, the relationship is somewhat deeper than that. Our guardian angel was created out of the same essence that makes up our soul. It could be said to be a higher or *essence* aspect of our self. Guardian angels are also called tutelary angels because they stay with us, watching over our lives, protecting us, and encouraging our spiritual well-being and happiness.

Our guardian angels are not separate from us. They are dedicated to us and travel with us everywhere we go and are with us at all times. They have made an agreement with our soul to assist us in completing any of the tasks or lessons we have decided to undertake in each and every life. This is the reason why angels have been known to make miraculous rescues from accidents. For instance, if we have decided to remain here on Earth for a given length of time, our angel will assist us if we are in a situation where we might transition earlier than our allotted time. It may be that we have certain contributions still left to make or lessons that we have not yet learned. We agreed on an exit date, but due to free will or changes in our plan with our higher self, angels, and guides, our angels can arrange to give us more time if it is necessary. These changes will only be made if it is for our highest good, the higher good of humanity, or the higher good of the soul group involved.

It is important to remember that we agreed to assume specific situations in our lives. For example, we may agree to pass over from cancer. We may agree to have a life where we lose an arm, leg, or maybe even our eyesight, or we may agree to an early exit date where we may pass in a car wreck at a young age. The only thing that matters is that we learn or attempt to learn our lessons before our exit date. Death shouldn't be feared, especially since there is no such thing as death. We are born into cycles of reincarnation and karma and rejoin our soul groups for review in between our earthbound life experiences. If we have a child dying of cancer or one who died in a car crash, that child chose his/her time and manner of death. We may feel incredibly sad, but there will be lessons for all involved in these situations. There are no accidents in our lives.

Angels are centered within the heart of the Divine. They are in God's presence and grace at all times. An angel is created to serve, love, hold, and guide those to whom they are assigned and those who ask for angelic support.

Angels can be found in every corner of the universe and are countless in numbers. If we could see angels with the naked eye, we would be amazed at just how populated the Earth really is. There are many amazing and wonderful beings here, helping our Earth and the people on it, even though they may not be visible for all to see.

We can see, feel, and hear our angels at any time if we just calm our minds and try to listen. They are above us, below us, over our shoulders, or next to us at all times. They will never stop trying to reach us and give us messages that we are not alone, and they are here trying to help. Our angels are that part of our eternal being that is holding our vision and focus for us even when we are not.

Our angels have love and protection to impart, and, as such, their purpose is to provide us with a reflection of our true nature so that we may never really forget our connection with the Divine. Our angels hold the blueprint of what we truly are so that we may awaken to our ultimate truth.

There are angels for every function we can think of, and then some. There is no limit to how many angels we can have in our life, and there is no limit to how many we can ask for at any particular moment. We can ask angels to assist us with any project, problem, or issue we may have. We can call upon our angels whenever we wish and for whatever purpose we want, provided that the purpose is not intended to hurt or injure anyone or anything.

We can ask our angels to fill our home with love, watch over our children at school, travel with us on long journeys, aid us when we are trying to stop smoking, or help us to stay focused when we are trying to lose weight and get healthier. We can ask an angel to take care of our computer or to assist us in resolving an argument with a friend or relative. By asking angels to be present everywhere in our life, we will begin to embody angelic qualities. We will be more open to the love and abundance of the universe. We will begin to experience more joy, health, and laughter as we sense the wings of angels flying around every aspect of our life.

Archangels are high ranking angels that are found in the second choir of angels. A choir is the name used for the order of angels, a method of organization that proposes a kind of celestial group for the entire angelic realm. The term "choirs" is probably derived from one of the most central roles of all angels, the singing of praises to God so that all of heaven and creation will reverberate with joyous sound.

There are seven archangels that can be found in a number of religious traditions. They are as follows:

1. **Chamuel**: Archangel Chamuel is also known as Camael, Camiel, Camiul, Camniel, Cancel, Jahoel, Kemuel, Kahmael, Seraphiel, and Shemue. Chamuel is the archangel of adoration, love, and tolerance. His name means "He who sees God." He inspires us to realize that we must first love ourselves in order to love others. He gently guides us to view our own shortcomings. Chamuel helps us with world peace, our careers, lost items, and our life's purpose. He helps with relationships and can lift our spirit in the depths of sorrow to find love within our hearts.

2. **Gabriel**: Archangel Gabriel is also known as Abruel, Jibril, Jiburili, and Serafili. Gabriel is an angelic messenger. Her name means "Strength of God" or "The Divine is my strength." Of the seven archangels, Gabriel is the only archangel portrayed as a woman. Gabriel carries and instills love, truth, joy, justice, and grants wisdom in interpreting dreams and visions. She can guide us with our life purpose in arts and communication. Also, if our body needs detoxifying, Gabriel can purify both our body and our thoughts.

3. **Jophiel**: Archangel Jophiel is also known as Iofiel, Iophiel, Jofiel, and Zophiel. Jophiel is the archangel of creative power. This angel inspires us toward awareness, enlightenment, open-mindedness, and freedom of thought. He teaches our consciousness to discover the light within. His name means "Beauty of God" or "Divine Beauty." Jophiel is the patron of artists, helping with artistic projects and thinking beautiful thoughts. He can bring joy or laughter into our life and help us to seek the connection with our higher self so we can walk on our path to our higher spiritual purpose.

4. **Michael**: Archangel Michael is also known as Beshter, Mika'il, and Sabbathiel. Michael is the archangel of miracles. Michael is the most well-known archangel who strengthens our spirits during difficult times or dangerous situations. His name means "One who is like God," "Who is like God," or "Who is like the Divine." It is, however, meant to be a question: "Who is like the Lord?" Archangel Michael inspires truth, patience, and love. He is the one that leads our souls to heaven. He is the leader of the archangels and is in charge of protection, strength, courage, and truth. He is to rid the earth of fear and helps us to follow our

own inner truth without compromising our integrity. Archangel Michael gives us protection and strength in all areas of our lives.

5. **Raphael**: Archangel Raphael is also known as Labbiel. Raphael is the archangel of healing. He is known for extreme healing energy, which he bestows on everyone. His name means "Healing power of God," "Divine Healer," or "God who heals." In Hebrew, the word *rapha* means doctor or healer, and he is a powerful healer of all living forms, including humans and animals. Besides healing, he can grant us creativity, grace, joy, and love. He also encourages us to be self-motivated so we can become who we desire to be. He is said to be the most playful, friendly, and humorous of all the angels and can help guide us on our travels.

6. **Uriel**: Uriel is the archangel of creativity. His name means "Fire of God" or "Light of God." Uriel kindles and rekindles the spark within our heart that God created. He also rules over music and literature. Uriel helps us to embrace our own psychic and spiritual gifts. Uriel warned Noah of the impending flood and gives us prophetic information and warning in our lives. Uriel also helps to heal ourselves and the earth after earthquakes, floods, fires, tornados, or any other natural disasters.

7. **Raguel**: Archangel Raguel is also known as Akrasiel, Raguil, Rasuil, Rufael, and Suryan. Raguel is the archangel of the underdog. His name means "Friend of God." He oversees all other angels and archangels. We can call on him for help when we need to be empowered and respected. Raguel helps resolve arguments and creates harmony for family and friends.

Angels have been recognized by major religions as having an important place in the overall plan of creation. The following is a list of some of the more popular angels that are working with us and preparing us to ascend to higher levels of consciousness during our spiritual evolution:

Abdiel: Angel of Faith
Adnachiel: Angel of Independence
Afriel: Angel of Youth
Ambriel: Angel of Communications
Anael: Angel of Romantic Love
Anahita: Angel of Fertility
Anauel: Angel of Prosperity
Ananchel: Angel of Grace
Ariel: Angel of Nature
Armaita: Angel of Truth
Asmodel: Angel of Patience
Baglis: Angel of Moderation
Balthial: Angel of Forgiveness
Barakiel: Angel of Good Fortune
Barbelo: Angel of Goodness
Barchiel: Angel of Compassion
Bath Kol: Angel of Prophecy
Camael: Angel of Joy
Cassiel: Angel of Temperance
Cathetel: Angel of the Garden
Chamuel: Archangel of Adoration, Love, and Tolerance
Charmeine: Angel of Harmony
Charoum: Angel of Silence
Cherubim: Angel of Wisdom
Colopatiron: Angel of Liberation
Dina: Angel of Learning
Gabriel: Archangel of Communication, Messages, and
    Messengers
Galgaliel: Angel of Vibration
Gavreel: Angel of Peace

Gazardiel: Angel of New Beginnings
Haamiah: Angel of Integrity
Hadraniel: Angel of Love
Hael: Angel of Kindness
Hamael: Angel of Dignity
Hamaliel: Angel of Logic
Hamied: Angel of Miracles
Haniel: Angel of Harmonious Love
Harahel: Angel of Knowledge
Hayyel: Angel of Wild Animals
Iahhel: Angel of Meditation
Iofiel: Angel of Beauty
Isda: Angel of Nourishment
Israfel: Angel of Song
Jamaerah: Angel of Manifestation
Jehoel: Angel of Presence
Jophiel: Archangel of Creative Power
Kaeylarae: Angel of Peace
Kakabel: Angel of the Stars
Kutiel: Angel of Water
Lailah: Angel of Conception
Liwet: Angel of Invitations
Maion: Angel of Self-Discipline
Malahidael: Angel of Courage
Manakel: Angel of the Oceans
Melchizedek: Angel of Peace
Metatron: Angel of Thought
Micah: Angel of the Divine Plan
Michael: Archangel of Miracles and Protection
Mihael: Angel of Loyalty
Mihr: Angel of Friendship
Mumiah: Angel of Longevity
Muriel: Angel of Emotions
Nathaniel: Angel of Fire
Nemamiah: Angel of Just Cause
Nisroc: Angel of Freedom
Omniel: Angel of Oneness

Ongkanon: Angel of Communication
Ooniemme: Angel of Gratitude
Orifiel: Angel of Forests
Paschar: Angel of Vision
Perpetiel: Angel of Success
Qaphsiel: Angel of the Moon
Raguel: Archangel of God
Rampel: Angel of Endurance
Raphael: Archangel of Healing
Rashnu: Angel of Judgment
Raziel: Angel of Mysteries
Rahael: Angel of Self-Respect
Remliel: Angel of Awakening
Rhamiel: Angel of Empathy
Sachael: Angel of Water
Samandiriel: Angel of Imagination
Sandalphon: Angel of Power
Sariel: Angel of Guidance
Shekinah: Angel of Unity and Unconditional Love
Shemael: Angel of Gratitude
Shushienae: Angel of Purity
Sofiel: Angel of Nature
Soqed Hozi: Angel of Partnership
Sraosha: Angel of Obedience
Tabbris: Angel of Self-Determination
Taharial: Angel of Purification
Trgiaob: Angel of Wild Birds
Uriel: Archangel of Creativity
Urim: Angel of Light
Uzziel: Angel of Faith
Valoel: Angel of Peace
Verchiel: Angel of Affection
Vohamanah: Angel of Optimism
Pistis Sophia: Angel of Creation
Zacharael: Angel of Surrender
Zadkiel: Archangel of Prayer and Comfort
Zagzagel: Angel of Wisdom

Zuphlas: Angel of Trees
Zuriel: Angel of Harmony

Considering that we live in a materialistic world and need scientific and technological proof of most things in our universe, it is almost impossible to believe that we accept the existence of angels and their active presence in our lives without much thought. Those who believe in and acknowledge a spiritual realm are able to step beyond the boundaries of the physical world. For them, both faith and reason point to a spiritual dimension populated with angels.

Our greatest teachers, such as Buddha, tell us that the greatest strength is not obtained through great intellect or athletic ability but by faith. Through faith, we can find our greatest strength, inspiration, and the gift of and belief in our angels.

We should be aware that we are united with our angels and share a common mission with them—our spiritual growth and mastery. They abound all around us every day of our lives and stand by us during turbulent times. We need only ask for their help when needed. They have been here since the beginning of time and will always be here until the end of time to assist us with our spiritual evolution.

Chapter 12
A Spiritual Evolution

I shall tell you a great secret, my friend. Do not wait for the last judgment; it takes place every day.

~Albert Camus

*A*t every moment in our lives we make choices that will either lead us closer to or further away from remembering the spiritual essence we truly are. When we choose to awaken our true selves, we ascend further into higher dimensional consciousness as we progress on the path of our spiritual evolution. We have been in a spiritual evolution, as well as a biological evolution, throughout the span of space and time; that is, we have been evolving both spiritually and biologically. Our spiritual evolution is about growth of our being, the advancement of our souls, and the consciousness that resides within our spirits. Our awareness of who we are and why we are here is crucial to our spiritual evolutionary process. During our spiritual evolution, our consciousness and awareness must be constantly present in our journey, or we will become stagnant and fail to progress.

In spirit, evolving or ascending is a change in the inherited traits of our spirit from one generation to the next. These changes are caused by a combination of three processes: awareness, consciousness, and ascension.

Awareness is a term referring to our ability to perceive, to feel, or to be conscious of events, objects, or patterns. Awareness does not necessarily imply understanding nor does being aware mean that we are conscious. If we see a Coke can in a grocery store parking lot, we are aware that it is there. If we pick it up, bring it home, and put it in a recycling bin, then we are conscious of it.

People seeking their spiritual paths through awareness are curious about themselves and the things around them. People of expanded spiritual awareness often become engaged in improving the welfare of humanity and the environment in one way or another. In the end, we will come to realize that if we expand our awareness, we can change our lives for the better on many levels of our being.

Our spiritual awareness or spiritual awakening is the process by which we begin to explore our own being in order to become whole and reunited with our true spiritual meaning. As we become more spiritually aware, we realize that we live by the Law of One. This law reminds us to look for the commonalities we have with each other and not the differences. It encourages us to build bridges that show us that we are all connected. Awareness of who and what we are opens the way for our spiritual evolution and an expansion beyond our current and outdated beliefs.

The greatest gift of living a life in awareness is knowing that our spirit never dies. We have absolute freedom to experience everything that life has to offer in all of its full glory. It is said that it is not the destination in life but the journey that makes us who we are. The trip itself is not about knowing but about experiencing. These experiences are our only purpose; they are what life is. It is in living each physical life and the experiences it has to offer that is crucial for us to advance in our spiritual lessons and our spiritual evolution. This is done through our awareness.

We are not pawns or victims in our awareness; we are the creators and the created. In this knowledge or awareness, we can find comfort in knowing that the joy of our lives, the joy of living, is nothing more than a buffet of experiences that we can choose from. These experiences, good or bad, give us opportunity to expand not just our awareness but also our knowledge and wisdom.

As we become spiritually aware, all things in our lives have an opportunity to change and evolve. The beauty of our spiritual evolution and spiritual experiences is that they are a doorway for unlimited new opportunities and new experiences. These opportunities and experiences are presented to us every day of our lives. Whether we chose to learn and grow from them is up to us.

Awareness is also about realizing our God and Goddess selves and creating heaven on Earth. It is about embracing who we really are and dispelling the thought that we are separate from our Creator or the Divine. It is about bringing the higher and lower aspects of our being into complete harmony and alignment with our higher self or higher purpose in life.

Awareness has ramifications for us on this physical world of mind, body, and soul. Physics tells us that everything is composed of energy. Even if we can't see it, energy exists at various frequencies, and is, in essence, all things. Our bodies are essential in maintaining the harmony between our physical body and our soul. If we are not aware of how to treat, feed, and honor our bodies, then we will have a more difficult time raising our vibrational frequencies.

Our ultimate goal in spiritual awareness is to align with a higher source and keep our vibrational frequencies at a higher level to help us live out our life's purpose and find the special gifts and talents that we have to offer. Living a life in awareness can be done in many ways. Prayer, meditation, reading, and practicing good karma are all ways to help raise our vibrational frequency and awareness. By calming our minds, expanding our knowledge, and working on our spiritual lessons, we can bring ourselves closer to the spiritual mastery we are seeking to obtain with each life that we live.

Living our life's purpose is another way to be aware. People often ask, "What is my life's purpose?" Our life's purpose can be learned by communication with our guides and angels. By raising vibrational frequencies to a higher level, it becomes easier to communicate with our higher self, our guides, and our angels who are here loving us and helping us to discover our life's purpose. Our angels and guides work hard on helping us discover who we are, why we are here, and what gifts and talents we have to offer humanity and our Earth.

For most of us, it can take up to half our lifetimes to wake up to the fact that we have a mission or a purpose while here on Earth. Feeling that something is coming or that we have some big mission to accomplish is quite common among those of us who are waking up and becoming aware of who we are and why we are here. For many of us, there is a constant underlying feeling or thought that we should be doing something bigger or more important with our lives. That we have something special to contribute that is bigger than ourselves.

Our awareness allows us to be treated as the unique souls that we are. We are all becoming more aware, whether we realize it or not. Awareness will make it possible for all life to blossom and for all of us to manifest our dreams, live our life's purpose, and experience the life intended for all souls. By being aware, we move into higher dimensional consciousness and more forward in our spiritual evolution. In time, through awareness, unity will allow all life to stand with compassion, love, respect, and a value of wholeness and oneness. This idea is so simplistic in its value but seemingly difficult for us to execute. Through our awareness we will be able to expand in our knowledge, grow in our wisdom, and become the enlightened beings we are capable of being.

Consciousness is another process in which we are participating in a spiritual evolution. As we sweep into the 21st century, we are becoming more spiritual, seeking divinity and knowledge of our inner worlds and looking for answers to the purpose of our existence.

Most of us feel that a higher power exists and that we are all connected to a Divine source of some kind. Many of us in the world today are focusing on spiritual development and attaining enlightenment in growing numbers. We will soon come to realize through our consciousness that we all worship the same God in different forms and approaches, and we are all of the same essence. There will be a time when we recognize a great conscious awakening among us all, one where life will be lived without war and hatred but, instead, lived with love and compassion.

Consciousness is a difficult term to define because the word is used and understood in a wide variety of ways. What frequently happens is one person's definition of consciousness is seen by others as something else altogether. Consciousness may involve thoughts, sensations, perceptions, moods, emotions, dreams, and self-awareness. Sometimes consciousness denotes being awake and responsive to ourselves and our environment in contrast to being unconscious and unaware. In the end, consciousness is about acting with awareness and being in an awakened state. It is about physically making changes, however trivial they may seem, with thoughtfulness and compassion. Our decisions should be made in consciousness of a picture greater than just ourselves.

In order to be in a place of higher dimensional consciousness, we must become fully conscious. This means stopping old patterns and habits that prevent us from living in heightened awareness. Our archaic systems no longer serve the good of humanity, and we must stop and change these systems or we will fail on a global level. These changes will bring us into the light of higher conscious awareness. There are many means for bringing limited aspects of ourselves into the light of higher consciousness, and angels are tirelessly working on this to help us.

If we talk about spirit in a conscious manner, we refer to our level of perception about ourselves and the world around us. That is, the higher the perception, the greater the consciousness. The angels say that if over 50% of the population is conscious about something, it can be changed. When working consciously on issues, it doesn't mean we are just thinking about it. Again, it means we are doing something about it. As we have been shifting ourselves to enlightenment through our spiritual evolution, we are already beginning to see great changes that are happening for the better here on Earth and, unfortunately, some for the worse. If our issue or issues lie with ourselves, our families, our cities, or our countries, the bottom line is we should never stop trying to change. There are no tasks that cannot be overcome, no matter how large or daunting they may seem.

One of the most common experiences of spiritual consciousness is the feeling of oneness. Oneness is often experienced as a feeling that everything is part of a whole or that we all come from one common source, share a common spirit, and are all connected. If we hurt someone, something, or the environment—we are only hurting ourselves.

The spiritual experience of oneness is expressed by the perception that there is a level of consciousness that transcends our normal experience of what is good and what is bad. A person normally accepts good things that happen in life as well as bad things that happen. Through the unitary spiritual experience of oneness, we rise to a higher level of consciousness and come to understand that the difference between good and bad is not what we normally perceive. They are both beneficial to us in some way.

The bad things that happen to us in life serve a very important purpose: that purpose is to help us and the world around us with our spiritual evolution. If we look at challenging situations in our lives, we can understand that at the end of our life's work, both our good and bad experiences are all for our highest good. Conversely, through the experience of spiritual consciousness, we begin to see that many things we perceive as good may not be truly good and may just be expressions of our desires, attachments, preferences, or karmic balancing.

We can all look back over the course of our lives and see that the difficult circumstances we have experienced were often a doorway to a new beginning or opportunity.. If we can carry into our daily lives a consciousness that goes beyond good and bad, we will be able to operate from a more centered platform. This will enable us to make better decisions for ourselves and grow from our experiences as we see our world with greater and deeper insights.

Spiritual consciousness can be maintained on a daily basis by beginning each day with this thought: "Today my every word, thought, and action will be as my angels, guides, or higher power would want for my highest good." This simple reminder will keep us conscious of our spiritual principles that we should be incorporating into our lives, such as the Law of One and the Golden Rule.

Our own consciousness is a reflection of the development of our spirit. Understanding the reason for our human existence gives rise to understanding why we go through various positive or negative experiences, why lessons continue to repeat themselves within our lives, and why we must learn to overcome our fears and resistances versus remaining a victim to ourselves and these fears.

The relationship to our own consciousness is a direct relationship to the development of our spiritual evolution. Our spiritual evolution is why we are here and why we have been coming back here over and over again. Living our lives in consciousness will always bring us closer to this process and our spiritual mastery.

Ascension is the third process in our spiritual evolution. If ascending is evolving, then ascension is, indeed, evolution. We are all ascending into higher dimensional consciousness as a civilization and are in the midst of an incredibly powerful spiritual evolution through our ascension.

Through the process of ascension and our spiritual evolution, it is important to recognize that our ego is not beneficial for us—that it causes much unneeded and unwanted suffering. Our spiritual truth asks the question "How much suffering will it take for us to recognize who we are, why we are here, and to join hands as brothers and sisters of humanity?" Ego operates out of fear and robs us of our peace and wholeness. With ascension, decisions in our lives should be made from the heart and a state of compassion. This will allow us to raise our vibrational frequency and grow in our spiritual lessons and spiritual evolution.

Our world is ascending to higher dimensional consciousness, and we as her children must ascend with our Earth, or our Earth will make us change. Mother Nature will execute her plan one way or another in our ascension or shift. If we continue to ascend, we can avoid catastrophes, whether social, ecological, military, environmental, or others, which will force us to change with our world if we do not change with her.

The development of own awareness, consciousness, and ascension has a direct relationship to the development of our spiritual evolution. We can arise and awaken within our consciousness our memories of all lives we have lived. We can arise and awaken to our true meaning and our true spiritual purpose. We can arise and awaken to the joys and wonders of this life and our spiritual evolution.

Nikki Pattillo graduated from Stephen F. Austin State University in Texas and began her career as a clinical and molecular biologist. She is the author of Children of the Stars: Advice for Parents and Star Children and also writes numerous newspaper articles to help raise awareness in consciousness on both environmental and spiritual issues.

As a child, Nikki was psychic conversing regularly with her angels and guides. This natural gift was not understood by her family or friends and consequently she shut down her abilities out of fear. It was these same angels and guides that came to her later in life and said that it was time for her to allow her gifts to grow stronger and open a path for others, especially children, to follow in peace and harmony and without fear of their gifts.

Children of the Stars: Advice for Parents and Star Children was written as a guide to help parents understand their Star children and to help each parent spiritually understand what is happening with these gifted children who are here to help us. It was written to help children understand and not be fearful of seeing and hearing things that others cannot see or hear.

Nikki says, "The most wonderful aspect of Star children is their willingness to take on the world and learn to make their own way through it. Star children will get to the point where they are able to mold society into something that reflects their energies and values. The truth that they hold and defend so well will reflect their integrity and spirituality and change the world as we know it."

Other Books Published
by
Ozark Mountain Publishing, Inc.